AAT

The Business Environment Synoptic Assessment

Pocket Notes

These Pocket Notes support study for the following AAT qualifications:

AAT Level 2 Certificate in Accounting

AAT Level 2 Certificate in Bookkeeping

AAT Certificate in Accounting at SCQF Level 6

British library cataloguing-in-publication data

A catalogue record for this book is available from the British Library.

Published by:
Kaplan Publishing UK
Unit 2 The Business Centre
Molly Millars Lane
Wokingham
Berkshire
RG41 2QZ

ISBN 978-1-83996-904-1

© Kaplan Financial Limited, 2024

Printed and bound in Great Britain.

CONTENTS

Business Environment

Preface

These Pocket Notes contain the key things that you need to know for the exam, presented in a unique visual way that makes revision easy and effective.

Written by experienced lecturers and authors, these Pocket Notes break down content into manageable chunks to maximise your concentration.

Quality and accuracy are of the utmost importance to us so if you spot an error in any of our products, please send an email to mykaplanreporting@kaplan.com with full details, or follow the link to the feedback form in MyKaplan.

Our Quality Co-ordinator will work with our technical team to verify the error and take action to ensure it is corrected in future editions.

A guide to the assessment

The assessment

The synoptic assessment is a compulsory component of the AAT Level 2 Certificate and Diploma qualification. It combines elements of learning outcomes from the following units into a scenario-based assessment:

- Introduction to Bookkeeping
- Principles of Bookkeeping Controls
- Business Environment

Not all of the learning outcomes of the above units are assessable in the synoptic assessment.

Based upon the specimen assessments released by AAT, the synoptic assessment will comprise eight tasks, and will be for two hours. The synoptic assessment is partially human-marked and partially computer-marked.

Pass mark

To pass an assessment, students need to achieve a mark of 70% or more.

Scope of content

The syllabus for the synoptic assessment comprises eight Assessment Objectives based upon the learning objectives of the underlying units as follows:

Assessment Objective	Weighting
A01 Demonstrate an understanding of the different business types and their functions	10%
A02 Demonstrate an understanding of the finance function, its information requirements and sources, and its role in the wider organisation	13%
A03 Demonstrate an understanding of corporate social responsibility (CSR), ethics and sustainability	14%
A04 Process bookkeeping transactions and communicate information	22%
A05 Produce and reconcile control accounts, and use journals to correct errors	10%
A06 Demonstrate an understanding of the principles of contract law	7%
A07 Demonstrate an understanding of bookkeeping systems, receipts and payments, and the importance of information and data security	10%
A08 Demonstrate an understanding of the global business environment	14%
Total	**100%**

Composition of assessment objectives

Assessment objective 1	Demonstrate an understanding of the different business types and their functions
Related learning outcomes	**The Business Environment** LO4 Understand the impact of setting up different types of business entity LO5 Understand the finance function within an organisation
Assessment objective 2	Demonstrate an understanding of the finance function, its information requirements and sources, and its role in the wider organisation
Related learning outcomes	**The Business Environment** LO5 Understand the finance function within an organisation LO6 Produce work in appropriate formats and communicate effectively LO7 Understand the importance of information to business operations
Assessment objective 3	Demonstrate an understanding of corporate social responsibility (CSR), ethics and sustainability
Related learning outcomes	**The Business Environment** LO3 Understand key principles of corporate social responsibility (CSR), ethics and sustainability

Assessment objective 4	Process bookkeeping transactions and communicate information
Related learning outcome	**Introduction to Bookkeeping** LO1 Understand how to set up bookkeeping systems LO2 Process customer transactions LO3 Process supplier transactions **The Business Environment** LO6 Produce work in appropriate formats and communicate effectively
Assessment objective 5	Produce and reconcile control accounts, and use journals to correct errors
Related learning outcome	**Principles of Bookkeeping Controls** LO1 Use control accounts LO2 Reconcile a bank statement with the cash book LO3 Use the journal

Assessment objective 6	Demonstrate an understanding of the principles of contract law
Related learning outcomes	**The Business Environment** LO1 Understand the principles of contract law
Assessment objective 7	Demonstrate an understanding of bookkeeping systems, receipts and payments, and the importance of information and data security
Related learning outcomes	**The Business Environment** LO7 Understand the importance of information to business operations **Introduction to Bookkeeping** LO1 Understand how to set up bookkeeping systems LO2 Process customer transactions LO3 Process supplier transactions **Principles of Bookkeeping Controls** LO1 Use control accounts LO2 Reconcile a bank statement with the cash book LO3 Use the journal

Assessment objective 8	Demonstrate an understanding of the global business environment
Related learning outcomes	**The Business Environment** LO2 Understand the external business environment

1

Books of prime entry

- Introduction.
- Sales day book.
- Sales returns day book.
- Purchases day book.
- Purchases returns day book.
- Cash receipts book.
- VAT.
- Cash payments book.
- Discounts allowed day book.
- Discounts received day book.
- Petty cash book.

Introduction

Rather than entering each individual transaction into the ledger accounts as they happen, books of prime entry are used to record transactions/documents of the same type before they are processed further.

KAPLAN PUBLISHIN

Sales day book

- list of invoices sent out to credit customers
- date
- invoice number
- customer name/account code
- invoice total analysed into net, VAT and gross (total)

- information copied from sales invoices
- before further processing, must be totalled
- totals can be checked by cross casting £3,794.14 + £758.82 = £4,552.96.

Sales Day book						
Date	Invoice No	Customer Name	Receivables ledger code	Total (gross) £	VAT (20%) £	Net £
12/08/X3	69489	TJ Builder	RL21	2,004.12	334.02	1,670.10
12/08/X3	69490	McCarthy & Sons	RL08	1,485.74	247.62	1,238.12
12/08/X3	69491	Trevor Partner	RL10	1,063.10	177.18	885.92
				4,552.96	758.82	3,794.14

Analysed sales day book

Sometimes the net figure (actual sales) is analysed into different types of sale/product type.

| Sales day book | | | | | | | | | | |
Date	Invoice No	Customer Name	Code	Total (gross) £	VAT £	Russia £	Poland £	Spain £	Germany £	France £
15/08/X1	167	Worldwide News	W5	3,000.00	500.00					2,500.00
	168	Local News	L1	240.00	40.00			200.00		
	169	The Press Today	P2	360.00	60.00				300.00	
	170	Home Call	H1	240.00	40.00			200.00		
	171	Tomorrow	T1	120.00	20.00					100.00
	172	Worldwide news	W5	3,600.00	600.00	3,000.00	–			
				7,560.00	1,260.00	3,000.00	–	400.00	300.00	2,600.00

Sales returns day book

- list of credit notes sent out to credit customers
- date
- credit note number
- customer name/account code
- credit note total analysed into net, VAT and total
- information copied from credit note.

SALES RETURNS DAY BOOK						
Date	Credit Note No.	Customer Name	Code	Total (gross) £	VAT £	Net £
28/08/X3	03561	Trevor Partner	RL10	125.48	20.91	104.57
28/08/X3	03562	TJ Builder	RL21	151.74	25.29	126.45
				277.22	46.20	231.02

Purchases day book

- list of invoices received from credit suppliers
- date
- purchase invoice number (often internal consecutive number allocated)
- supplier name/account code
- invoice total analysed into net, VAT and total (gross)
- information copied from purchase invoice
- before further processing, must be totalled
- totals can be checked by cross casting £663.90 + £132.77 = £796.67.

			PURCHASES DAY BOOK			
Date	Invoice No.	code	supplier	Total (gross) £	VAT £	Net £
20X1						
7 May	2814	PL06	J Taylor	190.41	31.73	158.68
8 May	2815	PL13	McMinn Partners	288.14	48.02	240.12
	2816	PL27	D B Bros	96.54	16.09	80.45
9 May	2817	PL03	J S Ltd	221.58	36.93	184.65
				796.67	132.77	663.90

Analysed purchases day book

Sometimes the net figure (actual purchases) is analysed into different types of purchase/product type.

			PURCHASES DAY BOOK						
Date	Invoice no	Code	Supplier	Total (gross) £	VAT £	01 £	02 £	03 £	04 £
05/02/X5	1161	053	Calderwood & Co	20.16	3.36	16.80			
05/02/X5	1162	259	Mellor & Cross	112.86	18.81		94.05		
05/02/X5	1163	360	Thompson Bros Ltd	42.86	7.14	35.72			

Purchases returns day book

- list of credit notes received from credit suppliers
- date
- credit note number (often internal consecutive number allocated)
- supplier name/account code
- credit note total analysed into net, VAT and total
- information copied from credit note.

PURCHASES RETURNS DAY BOOK

Date	Credit note no	Supplier	Code	Total (gross) £	VAT £	Net £
09/05/X1	02456	McMinn Partners	PL13	64.80	10.80	54.00
09/05/X1	02457	J S Ltd	PL03	72.00	12.00	60.00
				136.80	22.80	114.00

Cash receipts book

The cash receipts book records all money received into the business bank account for whatever reason.

Cash receipts book						
Date	Narrative	Total £	VAT £	Receivables £	Cash sales £	Sundry £
3 Jul	A Brown	20.54	3.42		17.12	
5 Jul	S Smith & Co Ltd	9.30		9.30		
	P Priest	60.80		60.80		
	James & Jeans	39.02	6.50		32.52	
	LS Moore	17.00		17.00		
6 Jul	L White Ltd	5.16		5.16		
7 Jul	M N Furnishers Ltd	112.58				112.58
	R B Roberts	23.65		23.65		
	Light and Shade	86.95		86.95		
		375.00	9.92	202.86	49.64	112.58

Date of receipt — Details of receipt — Total of receipts — Total VAT on cash sales — Total receipts from receivables — Total receipt for cash sales — Total receipts from sundry income

- entries to the cash receipts book come from either the remittance list or a photocopy of the paying in slip
- to check the totalling the cross casts should be checked:

	£
VAT	9.92
Receivables	202.86
Cash sales	49.64
Sundry income	112.58
Total	375.00

VAT

- VAT is only ever recorded in the cash receipts book on cash sales or other income
- any VAT on sales on credit (i.e. receipts from receivables) has already been recorded in the sales day book and posted to the ledger accounts from there.

Cash payments book

The cash payments book records all money paid out of the business bank account for whatever reason.

Date	Details	Cheque No	Total	VAT	Payables ledger £	Cash	Post
14/2	K Ellis	1152	80.00		80.00		
15/2	Hutt Ltd	1153	120.00	20.00		100.00	
16/2	Biggs Ltd	1154	200.00				200.00
			400.00	20.00	80.00	100.00	200.00

Date of payment	Details of payment	Total of payment	Total VAT on cash purchases	Total payment to payables	Total payment for cash purchases	Total payment for post

- entries to the cash payments book come from either the cheque stubs or other banking documentation.
- to check the totalling the cross casts should be checked:

	£
VAT	20.00
Purchases ledger	80.00
Cash purchases	100.00
Post	200.00
Total	400.00

VAT is only ever recorded in the cash payments book on cash purchases, or other payments for expenditure that attract VAT, which have not been entered in the purchases day book.

- any VAT on purchases on credit (i.e. payments to payables) has already been recorded in the purchases day book and posted to the ledger accounts from there.

KAPLAN PUBLISHIN

Discounts allowed day book

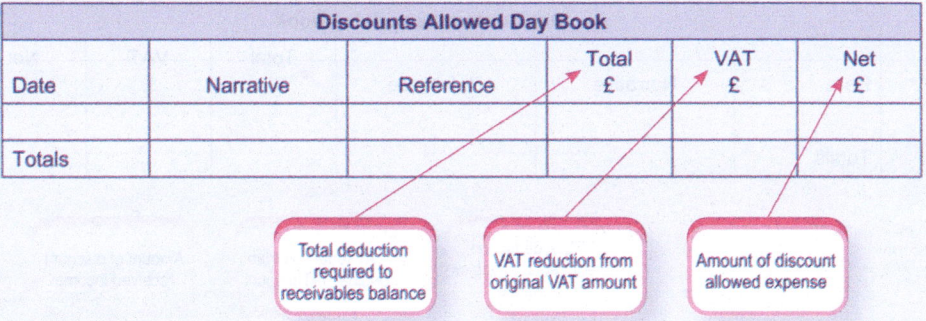

Discounts Allowed Day Book					
Date	Narrative	Reference	Total £	VAT £	Net £
Totals					

Total deduction required to receivables balance

VAT reduction from original VAT amount

Amount of discount allowed expense

The discounts allowed day book records the credit notes issued due to a customer taking advantage of a prompt payment discount.

Discounts received day book

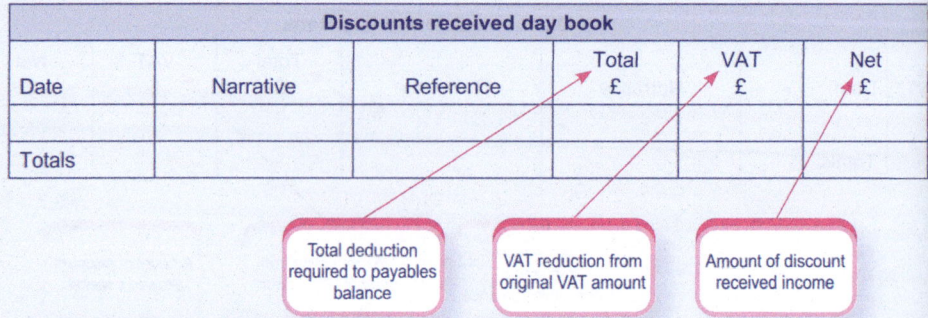

Discounts received day book					
Date	Narrative	Reference	Total £	VAT £	Net £
Totals					

Total deduction required to payables balance

VAT reduction from original VAT amount

Amount of discount received income

The discounts received day book records the credit notes received from a supplier due to us taking advantage of a prompt payment discount.

Petty cash book

- book of prime entry
- often part of general ledger as well
- small cash receipts side
- larger analysed cash payments side.

Receipts side – only one column as only entry is regular payment in cash from bank

Payments side – analysed according to typical expenditure plus VAT column

PETTY CASH BOOK

RECEIPTS			PAYMENTS								
Date	Narrative	Total £	Date	Narrative	Voucher no	Total £	Postage £	Cleaning £	Tea & Coffee £	Sundry £	VAT £
1 Nov	Bal b/f	35.50									
1 Nov	Cheque	114.50	1 Nov	ASDA	58	23.50			23.50		
			2 Nov	Post Office Ltd	59	29.50	29.50				
			2 Nov	Cleaning materials	60	15.07		12.56			2.51
			3 Nov	Postage	61	16.19	16.19				
			3 Nov	ASDA	62	10.57		8.81			1.76
			4 Nov	Newspapers	63	18.90				18.90	
			5 Nov	ASDA	64	12.10				10.09	2.01
						125.83	45.69	21.37	23.50	28.99	6.28

Imprest amount of £150 to start week

Date of claim

Details

Sequential petty cash voucher number

Analysed payments – total column includes VAT but analysis column amount is net of VAT

When petty cash book has been written up
for a period it must be totalled. Totals should
then be checked by cross-casting:

	£
Postage	45.69
Cleaning	21.37
Tea & coffee	23.50
Sundry	28.99
VAT	6.28
Total	125.83

2

Double entry bookkeeping – an introduction

- Principles of double entry bookkeeping.
- The accounting equation.
- Types of income and expense.

Principles of double entry bookkeeping

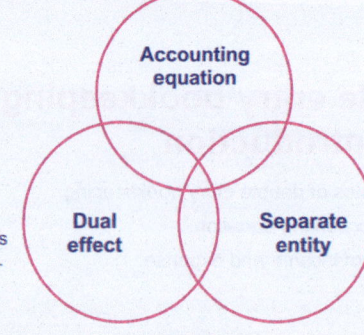

- each transaction has two financial effects.

Dual effect

Accounting equation

Separate entity

- the owner of the business is a separate entity from the business.

Therefore:

- each transaction has both a debit and a credit entry in the ledger accounts.

- the amount invested into the business by the owner is kept separate, it is known as "capital". The amount withdrawn from the business by the owner for their own personal use, it is known as "drawings".
- Note: capital and drawings are not necessarily just cash, an owner can invest and withdraw other assets.

Accounting equation

Assets – Liabilities = Capital

Terminology

Asset
- something owned by the business

Liability
- something owed by the business

Capital
- amount the owner has invested in the business

Receivable
- someone who owes the business money

Payable
- someone the business owes money to

The accounting equation

Accounting equation

(i) Ted pays £10,000 into a business bank account to start a business.

Dual effect	Assets (cash)	Capital
	£10,000	= £10,000

(ii) Ted buys goods to resell for £3,000 in cash

Dual effect	Assets + assets (cash) (inventory)	Capital
	£7,000 + £3,000	= £10,000

(iii) Ted sells the goods for cash for £4,000.

These goods were bought for £3,000, which is £1,000 less than what they have now been sold for. Therefore, a profit of £1,000 has been made.

This is added to the capital balance as it is an increase in the amount owed back to the owner of the business.

Dual effect	Assets (cash)	Capital	Profit
	£11,000	= £10,000 + £1,000

(iv) Ted purchases more goods for £6,000 on credit

Dual effect	Assets (inventory)	Liabilities (payable)	Capital + Profit
	£11,000 + £6,000	– £6,000	= £11,000

(v) Ted sells these goods for £8,000 on credit

Dual effect	Assets – Liabilities (receivables)	Capital + Profit
	£11,000 + £8,000 – £6,000	= £11,000 + £2,000

(vi) Ted pays £500 of rent for his premises. This reduces his cash and profit by £500

Dual effect	Assets (cash)	Capital + Profit
	£10,500 + £8,000 – £6,000	= £11,000 + £1,500

Chapter 2

Types of income and expense

Capital income

Income received from the sale of non-current assets

Example: The proceeds received from selling a motor vehicle

Revenue income

Income received from the trading activities

Example: The proceeds received from selling goods (inventory)

Capital expenditure

Expense of acquiring or improving non-current assets

Examples: Buying a piece of machinery, removing single glazed windows and replacing with double glazed windows

Revenue expenditure

Day to day running expenses of the business, including the repair and maintenance of non-current assets.

Examples: Gas, electricity, rent, repairs and maintenance

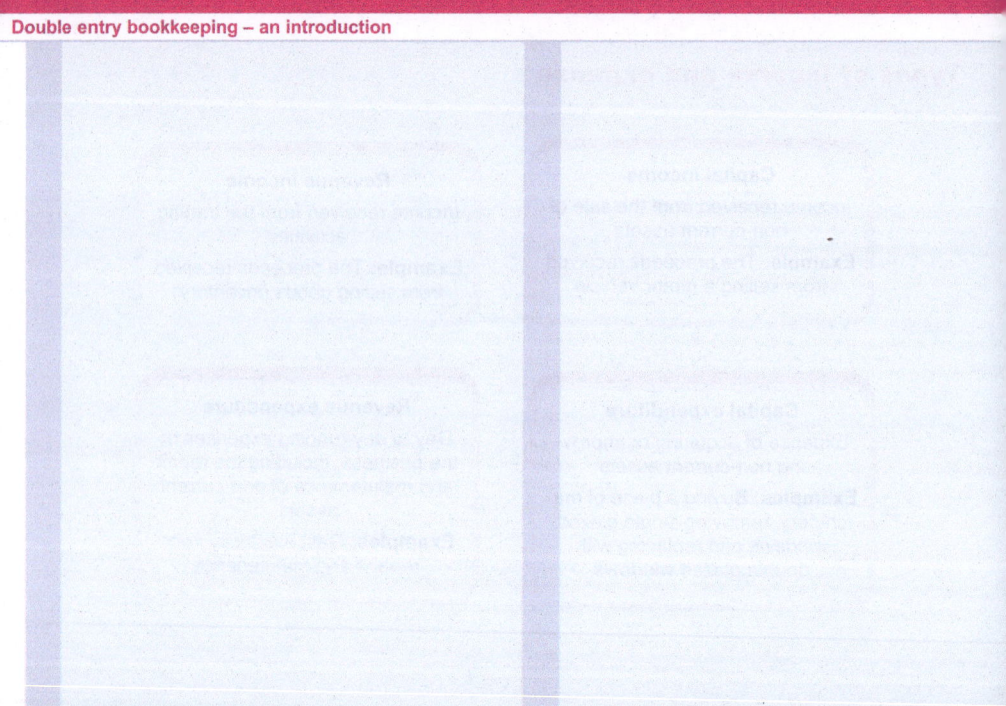

3

Ledger accounting

- Ledger accounts.
- General rules of double entry bookkeeping.
- Accounting for cash transactions.
- Accounting for credit transactions.
- Balancing the ledger accounts.
- What is a trial balance?

Ledger accounts

Typical ledger account:

Title of account

Date	Narrative	£	Date	Narrative	£
	DEBIT side			CREDIT side	

The dual effect means that every transaction has a debit entry in one account and a credit entry in another account.

Key question – which account is the debit entry in and which account is the credit entry in?

Definition

A **cash transaction** means a transaction which is paid for immediately.

Definition

A **credit transaction** is a transaction that is only paid after an agreed period of time, e.g. 30 days.

Note that the terms 'cash' and 'cheque' are used interchangeably in the early part of your studies. If the person pays by cash or cheque, the money will be entered into the 'bank' account (sometimes called the 'cash account').

Thus if John buys a car for £4,000 and pays immediately with a cheque or cash, that is a cash transaction.

If John buys a car for £4,000 on credit, when he eventually pays he can pay with either cash or a cheque – it makes no difference – it will be a credit transaction.

General rules of double entry bookkeeping

The table below summarises the effect a debit (DR) or a credit (CR) entry can have.

Ledger account

DEBIT	£	CREDIT	£
Money in		Money out	
Increase in asset		Increase in liability	
Decrease in liability		Decrease in asset	
Increase in expense		Increase in income	

The mnemonic **DEAD CLIC** is a great way to remember the side to post a debit or credit entry to.

DRs increase;	CRs increase;
Expenses	Liabilities
Assets	Income
Drawings	Capital

Accounting for cash transactions

Cash transactions

(i) Payment of £10,000 into business bank account by owner:
     Debit   Bank (money in)
     Credit Capital (increase in liability – amount owed to owner)

Bank account			
	£		£
Capital	10,000		

Capital account			
	£		£
		Bank	10,000

(ii) Purchase of goods for cash of £3,000
     Debit   Purchases (expense)
     Credit Bank (money out)

Purchases account			
	£		£
Bank	3,000		

Bank account			
	£		£
		Purchases	3,000

KAPLAN PUBLISHIN

(iii) Sale of goods for cash of £4,000
   Debit Bank (money in)
   Credit Sales (income)

Bank account				Sales account		
	£		£		£		£
Sales	4,000					Bank	4,000

(iv) Payment of rent in cash £500
   Debit Rent (expense)
   Credit Bank (money out)

Rent account				Bank account		
	£		£		£		£
Bank	500					Rent	500

Accounting for credit transactions

(i) Purchases goods for £6,000 on credit
    Debit   Purchases (expense)
    Credit Payables (liability)

Purchases account			
	£		£
Payables	6,000		

Payables account			
	£		£
		Purchases	6,000

(ii) Sale of goods on credit for £8,000
    Debit   Receivables (asset)
    Credit Sales (income)

Receivables account			
	£		£
Sales	8,000		

Sales account			
	£		£
		Receivables	8,000

(iii) Payment of part of money owed to credit supplier of £1,500

Debit   Payables (reduction in liability)
Credit Bank (money out)

Payables account			
	£		£
Bank	1,500		

Bank account			
	£		£
		Payables	1,500

(iv) Receipt of part of money owed by credit customer of £5,000

Debit   Bank (money in)
Credit Receivables (reduction in asset)

Bank account			
	£		£
Receivables	5,000		

Receivables account			
	£		£
		Bank	5,000

Balancing the ledger accounts

At various points in time the owner/owners of a business will need information about the total transactions in the period. E.g. total sales, amount of payables outstanding, amount of cash remaining. This can be found by balancing the ledger accounts.

Example

Here is a typical cash (or bank) account:

Cash account

	£		£
Capital	10,000	Purchases	3,000
Sales	4,000	Rent	500
Receivables	5,000	Payables	1,500

Step 1 Total both the debit side and the credit side and make a note of the totals.

Step 2 The higher of the totals should be inserted at the bottom of both the debit side and the credit side (leaving a line before inserting the totals).

Cash account

	£		£
Capital	10,000	Purchases	3,000
Sales	4,000	Rent	500
Receivables	5,000	Payables	1,500
	19,000		19,000

Step 3 On the side that amounts to the lower total, insert the figure that makes that side add up to the higher total. This balance should have the narrative "balance carried down" ("balance c/d").

Cash account

	£		£
Capital	10,000	Purchases	3,000
Sales	4,000	Rent	500
Receivables	5,000	Payables	1,500
		Balance c/d	14,000
	19,000		19,000

Step 4 On the opposite side to where the "balance carried down" has been inserted, enter the same figure below the total line. This should be referred to as "balance brought down" ("balance b/d").

Cash account

	£		£
Capital	10,000	Purchases	3,000
Sales	4,000	Rent	500
Receivables	5,000	Payables	1,500
		Balance c/d	14,000
	19,000		19,000
Balance b/d	14,000		

This shows that after all of these transactions there is £14,000 of cash left as an asset in the business (a debit balance brought down = an asset).

What is a trial balance?

- list of all of the ledger balances in the general ledger
- debit balances and credit balances listed separately
- debit balance total should equal credit balance total.

Trial balance

	Debit balances £	Credit balances £
Sales		5,000
Wages	100	
Purchases	3,000	
Rent	200	
Car	3,000	
Receivables	100	
Payables		1,400
	6,400	6,400

Debit or credit balance?

If you are just given a list of balances you must know whether they are debit or credit balances.

Remember the rules!

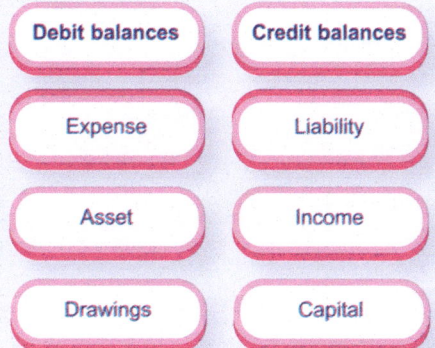

Debit balances	Credit balances
Expense	Liability
Asset	Income
Drawings	Capital

chapter

4

Accounting for credit sales, VAT and discounts

- Accounting for credit sales.
- VAT and discounts.
- Accounting for credit sales returns.

Accounting for credit sales

The double entry for a sale including VAT:

Dr	Receivables	X	(gross – VAT inclusive)
Cr	VAT (sales tax)	X	(VAT)
Cr	Sales	X	(net – VAT exclusive)

VAT and discounts

A trade discount or a bulk discount is a definite reduction to the list price of a product or service. These discounts will be deducted prior to VAT being calculated.

A prompt payment discount is merely offered to the customer on the invoice. No deduction to the invoice value or to the VAT calculation takes place until the customer takes advantage of this discount by making a payment within the required time.

Example

Goods are despatched to a customer with a list price of £1,000. The customer is allowed a trade discount of 20% and is offered a prompt payment discount of 4% if the invoice is paid within 10 days.

KAPLAN PUBLISHING

Invoice amounts:

	£
List price	1,000.00
Less: trade discount	(200.00)
	800.00
VAT (see below)	160.00
Invoice total	960.00
VAT calculation	£800 x 20%

NB The VAT has been calculated based on £800 (list price less trade discount).

Accounting for credit sales returns

The double entry for a sales return including VAT (sales tax) is:

Dr	Sales returns	X	(net – VAT exclusive)
Dr	VAT (sales tax)	X	(VAT)
Cr	Receivables	X	(gross – VAT inclusive)

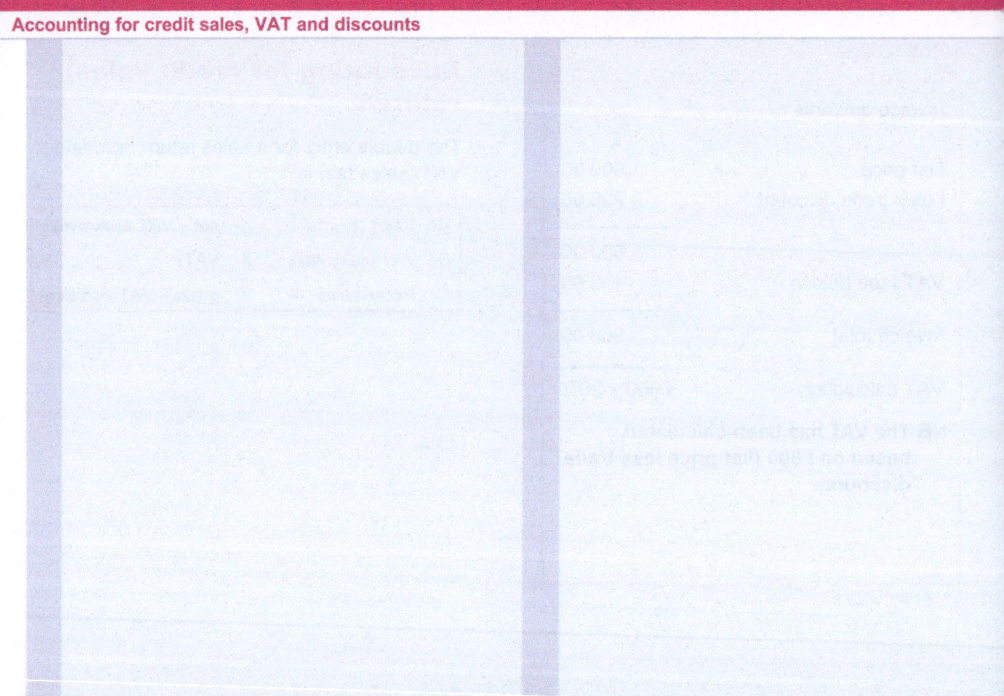

5

Accounting for credit purchases, VAT and discounts

- Accounting for credit purchases.
- VAT and discounts.
- Accounting for credit purchases returns.

Accounting for credit purchases

The double entry for a purchase including VAT:

Dr	Purchases	X	(net – VAT exclusive)
Dr	VAT (sales tax)	X	(VAT)
Cr	Payables	X	(gross – VAT inclusive)

VAT and discounts

VAT and discounts have already been studied when considering sales in chapter 4. The calculations of VAT and discounts are exactly the same when considering purchases.

The purchaser receives a "sales invoice" from the seller but the purchaser refers to this as a "purchase invoice" and enters it into the books accordingly. It is the same document but is referred to differently by the different parties involved in the transaction.

Ensure that you are happy with the calculations of VAT and discounts by reviewing over these in chapter 4.

Accounting for credit purchases returns

The double entry for a purchases return including VAT (sales tax) is:

Dr Payables	X	(gross – VAT inclusive)
Cr VAT (sales tax)	X	(VAT)
Cr Purchases returns	X	(net – VAT exclusive)

6

Control accounts and subsidiary ledgers

- Introduction.
- Receivables ledger control account.
- Posting the sales day book.
- Posting the sales returns day book.
- Payables ledger control account.
- Posting the purchases day book.
- Posting the purchases returns day book.

Introduction

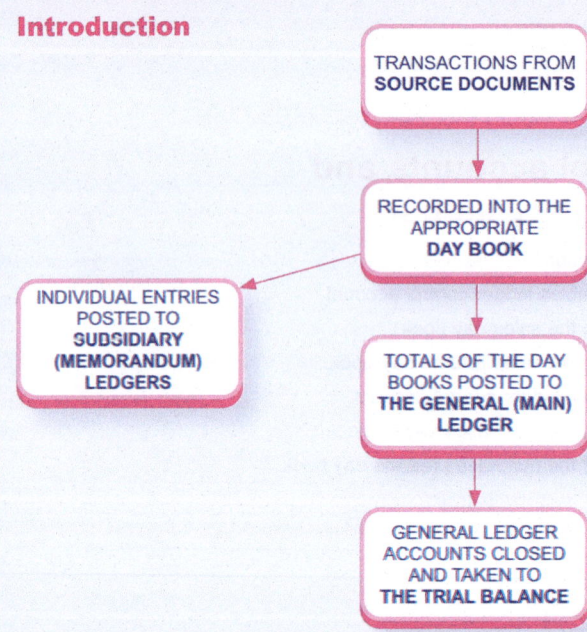

Receivables ledger control account

- total receivables account
- sales invoices posted from sales day book
- credit notes posted from sales returns day book
- receipts from customers posted from cash receipts book
- discounts allowed to customers posted from discounts allowed day book (or from the cash receipts book if no discounts allowed day book maintained).

Posting the sales day book

General ledger

- at the end of each day/week/month SDB is totalled
- totals must then be posted to accounts in the general ledger.

Double entry:

Debit	Receivables ledger Control account	Total (gross) figure
Credit	Sales account	Net figure
Credit	VAT account	VAT amount

SALES DAY BOOK

Date	Invoice No	Customer Name	Receivables ledger code	Total (gross) £	VAT £	Net £
12/08/X3	69489	TJ Builder	RL21	2,004.12	334.02	1,670.10
12/08/X3	69490	McCarthy & Sons	RL08	1,485.74	247.62	1,238.12
12/08/X3	69491	Trevor Partner	RL10	1,063.10	177.18	885.92
				4,552.96	758.82	3,794.14

Debit receivables ledger control account

Credit VAT

Credit sales

Receivables Ledger Control Account

	£		£
SDB	4,552.96		

Sales account

	£		£
		SDB	3,794.14

VAT

	£		£
		SDB	758.82

Subsidiary receivables ledger

- RLCA records the amount owing by all of the business's credit customers in total
- but also need information about each individual credit customer's balance
- therefore ledger account kept for each individual customer in a subsidiary ledger, the subsidiary receivables ledger.

Subsidiary receivables ledger

Customer A

£		£

Customer B

£		£

Customer C

£		£

Posting to the subsidiary receivables ledger

- each individual entry from the sales day book must be entered into the relevant customer account in the subsidiary receivables ledger
- amount entered is the gross invoice total (including VAT)
- entered on the debit side of the account indicating that this is the amount the receivable owes.

Example

Now we return to the sales day book from earlier and post the individual entries to the subsidiary receivables ledger.

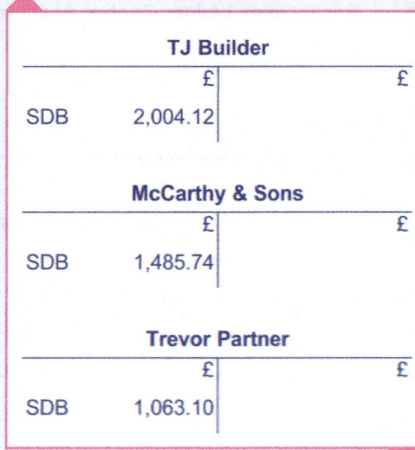

TJ Builder		
	£	£
SDB	2,004.12	

McCarthy & Sons		
	£	£
SDB	1,485.74	

Trevor Partner		
	£	£
SDB	1,063.10	

Posting the sales returns day book

General ledger

- as with the SDB the SRDB must also be posted to the general ledger accounts and subsidiary receivables ledger accounts.

Double entry:

Debit	Sales returns account	Net figure
Debit	VAT account	VAT total
Credit	Receivables Ledger Control Account	Total (gross) figure

SALES RETURNS DAY BOOK

Date	Credit Note No.	Customer Name	Code	Total (gross) £	VAT £	Net £
28/08/X3	03561	Trevor Partner	RL10	125.48	20.91	104.57
28/08/X3	03562	TJ Builder	RL21	151.74	25.29	126.45
				277.22	46.20	231.02

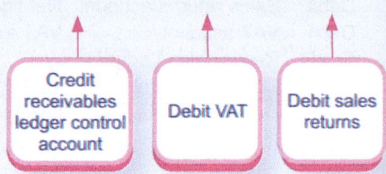

Credit receivables ledger control account

Debit VAT

Debit sales returns

Receivables ledger control account

	£		£
SDB	4,552.96	SRDB	277.22

Sales account

	£		£
		SDB	3,794.14

VAT account

	£		£
SRDB	46.20	SDB	758.82

Sales returns account

	£		£
SRDB	231.02		

Subsidiary receivables ledger

Each individual credit note must be entered in the customer's account:

- gross credit note total
- credit individual receivable account (reducing the amount owed).

T J Builder

	£		£
SDB	2,004.12	SRDB	151.74

McCarthy & Sons

	£		£
SDB	1,485.74		

Trevor Partner

	£		£
SDB	1,063.10	SRDB	125.48

Payables ledger control account

- total payables account
- purchase invoices posted from purchases day book
- credit notes posted from purchases returns day book
- payments to suppliers posted from cash payments book
- discounts received from suppliers posted from discounts received day book (or from cash payments book if no discount received day book maintained).

Posting the purchases day book (PDB)

General ledger

- at the end of each day/week/month PDB is totalled
- totals must then be posted to accounts in the general ledger.

Double entry:

Debit	Purchases account	Net figure
Debit	VAT account amount	VAT
Credit	Payables ledger Control account (PLCA)	Total (gross) figure

PURCHASES DAY BOOK

Date	Invoice No.	Code	Supplier	Total (gross) £	VAT £	Net £
20X1						
7 May	2814	PL06	J Taylor	190.41	31.73	158.68
8 May	2815	PL13	McMinn Partners	288.14	48.02	240.12
	2816	PL27	D B Bros	96.54	16.09	80.45
9 May	2817	PL03	J S Ltd	221.58	36.93	184.65
				796.67	132.77	663.90

Credit Payables ledger control account

Debit VAT

Debit purchases

Purchases account

	£		£
PDB	663.90		

VAT account

	£		£
PDB	132.77		

Payables ledger control account

	£		£
		PDB	796.67

Subsidiary payables ledger

- the PLCA records the amount owing to all of the business's credit suppliers in total
- but also need information about each individual credit supplier's balance
- therefore ledger account kept for each individual supplier in a subsidiary ledger, the subsidiary payables ledger.

Subsidiary Payables Ledger

Supplier A

£		£

Supplier B

£		£

Supplier C

£		£

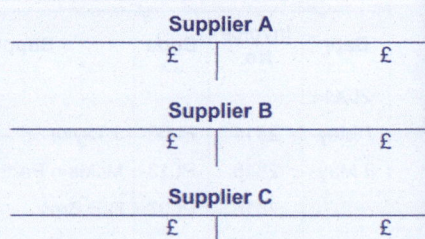

Posting to the subsidiary payables ledger

- each individual entry from the purchases day book must be entered into the relevant supplier account in the subsidiary payables ledger
- amount entered is the gross invoice total (including VAT)
- entered on the credit side of the account indicating that this is the amount owed to the supplier.

Example continued

Now we return to the purchases day book from earlier and post the individual entries to the subsidiary payables ledger.

J Taylor			
£			£
	PDB		190.41

D B Bros			
£			£
	PDB		96.54

McMinn Partners			
£			£
	PDB		288.14

J S Ltd			
£			£
	PDB		221.58

Posting the purchases returns day book (PRDB)

PURCHASES RETURNS DAY BOOK						
Date	Credit note no	Supplier	Code	Total (gross) £	VAT £	Net £
09/05/X1	02456	McMinn Partners	PL13	64.80	10.80	54.00
09/05/X1	02457	J S Ltd	PL03	72.00	12.00	60.00
				136.80	22.80	114.00

Debit Payables ledger control account

Credit VAT

Credit purchases returns

General ledger

- as with the PDB the PRDB must also be posted to the general ledger accounts and subsidiary payables ledger accounts.

Double entry:

Debit	Payables ledger Control account	Total (gross) figure
Credit	Purchases returns account	Net figure
Credit	VAT account total	VAT

Purchases account

	£		£
PDB	663.90		

VAT account

	£		£
PDB	132.77	PRDB	22.80

Payables Ledger Control Account

	£		£
PRDB	136.80	PDB	796.67

Purchases returns account

	£		£
		PRDB	114.00

Subsidiary payables ledger

Each individual credit note must be entered in the supplier's account:

- gross credit note total

debit individual supplier account (reducing the amount owing).

J Taylor

	£		£
		PDB	190.41

McMinn Partners

	£		£
PRDB	64.80	PDB	288.14

D B Bros

	£		£
		PDB	96.54

J S Ltd

	£		£
PRDB	72.00	PDB	221.58

7

Receipts and payments

- Receivables statements.
- Aged debt analysis.
- Posting the cash receipts book and the discounts allowed book to the general ledger.
- Posting the discounts allowed day book.
- Posting the cash receipts book and discounts allowed book to the subsidiary ledger.
- Checks to make on purchase invoices.
- Posting the cash payments book and discounts received book to the general ledger.

- Posting the discounts received day book.
- Posting the cash payments book and discounts received book to the subsidiary ledger.
- The cash book as part of the general ledger.
- Petty cash system.
- Petty cash vouchers.
- Petty cash book.
- Posting the petty cash book.
- Reconciling petty cash.
- Petty cash control account.
- Petty cash control account reconciliation.

Receivables' statements

- sent by supplier to customer usually monthly
- reminder of amounts due.

INVOICE				
Invoice to Fitch & Partners 23 Emma Place Manchester M6 4TZ		NICK BROOKS 225 School Lane Weymouth, Dorset WE36 5NR Tel: 0149 29381 Fax: 0149 29382 Date: 30/04/X2		
Date	Transaction	Debit £	Credit £	Balance £
03/04	INV001	185.65		185.65
10/04	CN001		49.35	136.30
14/04	INV005	206.80		343.10
18/04	PAYMENT		136.30	206.80
21/04	INV007	253.80		460.60
26/04	INV008	192.70		653.30
May we remind you that our credit terms are 30 days With 3% discount for payment within 14 days				

Aged debt analysis

- internal document
- prepared for each individual customer
- shows the age of amounts outstanding
- useful for identifying slow paying/problem customers.

Customer	Total £	<30 days £	30 to 60 days £	>60 days £
H Hardy	689.46	368.46	321.00	–
L Framer	442.79	379.60	–	63.19
K Knight	317.68	–	169.46	148.22

Posting the cash receipts book and the discounts allowed book to the general ledger

Basic double entry for cash receipts:

Debit	Bank account
Credit	Receivables Ledger Control Account (receipts from receivables)
	Sales (cash sales)
	Other income (e.g. rent)

In most cases the cash receipts book is not only a book of prime entry but also part of the general ledger in which case the debit entry for the total column is not required.

Double entry for discount allowed:

Debit	Discount allowed
Debit	VAT
Credit	Receivables Ledger Control Account

Postings

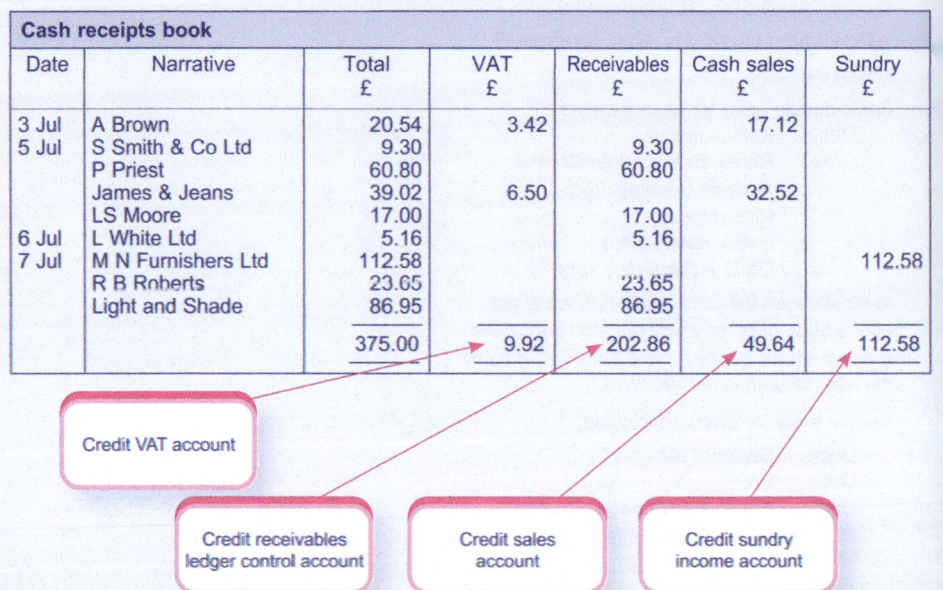

Cash receipts book						
Date	Narrative	Total £	VAT £	Receivables £	Cash sales £	Sundry £
3 Jul	A Brown	20.54	3.42		17.12	
5 Jul	S Smith & Co Ltd	9.30		9.30		
	P Priest	60.80		60.80		
	James & Jeans	39.02	6.50		32.52	
	LS Moore	17.00		17.00		
6 Jul	L White Ltd	5.16		5.16		
7 Jul	M N Furnishers Ltd	112.58				112.58
	R B Roberts	23.65		23.65		
	Light and Shade	86.95		86.95		
		375.00	9.92	202.86	49.64	112.58

Credit VAT account

Credit receivables ledger control account

Credit sales account

Credit sundry income account

Posting the discounts allowed day book

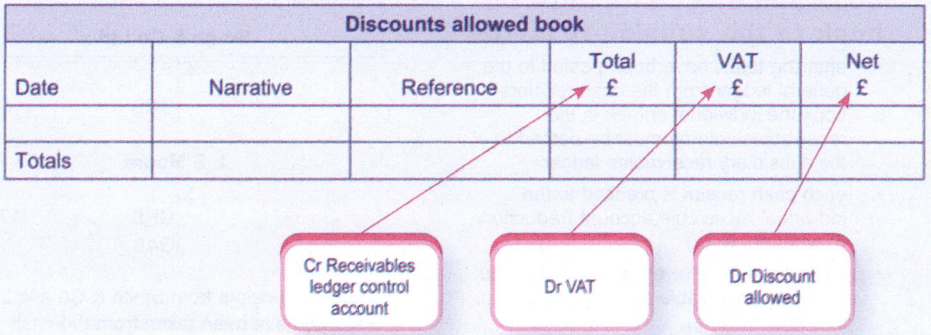

Discounts allowed book					
Date	Narrative	Reference	Total £	VAT £	Net £
Totals					

Cr Receivables ledger control account

Dr VAT

Dr Discount allowed

Posting the cash receipts book and discounts allowed book to the subsidiary ledger

- after the totals have been posted to the general ledger from the cash receipts book the individual entries in the receivables column must be posted to the subsidiary receivables ledger
- each cash receipt is credited to the individual receivable account (reduction of amount owing)
- each discount allowed is credited to the individual receivable account (reduction of amount owing).

Subsidiary receivables ledger – postings (extracts)

Smith & Co Ltd

£		£
	CRB	9.30

L S Moore

£		£
	CRB	17.00
	DAB	1.00

The cash receipts from Smith & Co and L S Moore have been taken from the cash receipts book. L S Moore received a prompt payment discount of £1.00 (gross).

Checks to make on purchase invoices

Once a purchase invoice is received from a supplier a number of checks must be made on it to ensure that it is valid before it is authorised for payment.

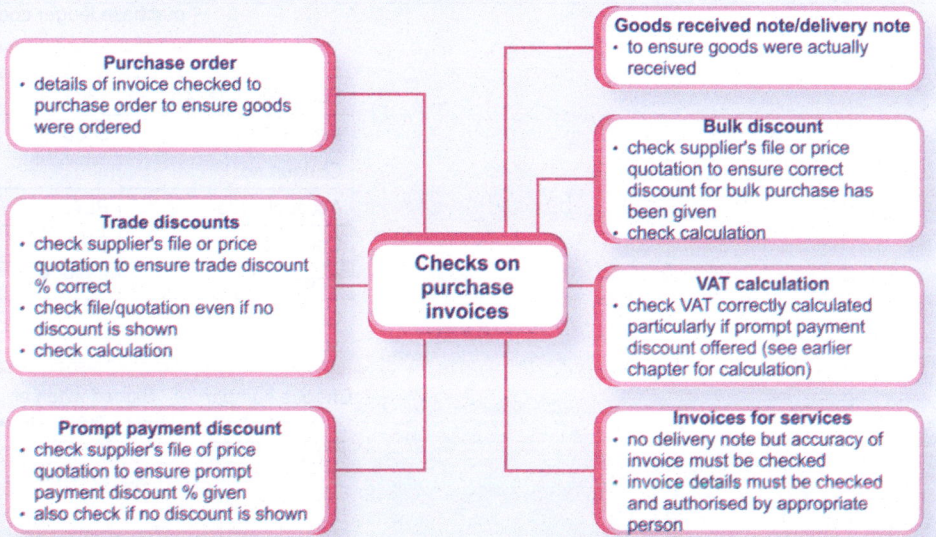

Purchase order
- details of invoice checked to purchase order to ensure goods were ordered

Trade discounts
- check supplier's file or price quotation to ensure trade discount % correct
- check file/quotation even if no discount is shown
- check calculation

Prompt payment discount
- check supplier's file of price quotation to ensure prompt payment discount % given
- also check if no discount is shown

Checks on purchase invoices

Goods received note/delivery note
- to ensure goods were actually received

Bulk discount
- check supplier's file or price quotation to ensure correct discount for bulk purchase has been given
- check calculation

VAT calculation
- check VAT correctly calculated particularly if prompt payment discount offered (see earlier chapter for calculation)

Invoices for services
- no delivery note but accuracy of invoice must be checked
- invoice details must be checked and authorised by appropriate person

Credit notes

The same checks as above should be made on credit notes received from suppliers.

Example of authorisation stamp

Account code is purchase ledger code

Purchase order no	436129
Invoice No	388649
Cheque no	
Account code	PL70
Checked	J Wilmber
Date	03/05/X4
General ledger account	

Cheque number inserted when payment made

Signed when all checks are made on invoice

When the invoice has been authorised, the amount to be paid must be calculated. This may also include accounting for prompt payment discount as considered previously.

Example

An invoice is received from a supplier as follows:

	£
List price	1,000.00
Trade discount	(200.00)
	800.00
VAT	160.00
	960.00

A 4% prompt payment discount is offered for payment within 14 days.

If the prompt payment discount is taken – the amount paid will be £960 less 4% which equals £921.60. This is made up of a revised net amount of £768 and a revised VAT charge of £153.60.

Payment by invoice
- each invoice paid at latest date allowed by credit terms
- must ensure that if the business policy is to take cash discounts then invoice is paid in time to reach supplier within agreed period

Payment on set date
- this may be one day per week/month but this may mean that cash discounts are lost
- alternative to set day per week/fortnight when all invoices which will have exceeded credit/settlement discount limit by following payment date are paid

Methods of scheduling of payments

Payment of supplier's statements
- received monthly showing invoices outstanding
- must be checked to supplier's account to ensure correct
- invoices on statement will be paid according to business policy
- often remittance advice attached to statement to show amounts being paid

Posting the cash payments book and the discounts received book to the general ledger

Basic double entry for cash payments :

Debit	Purchases for cash
Debit	Payables ledger control account
Debit	Other expenses
Credit	Bank account

In most cases the cash payments book is not only a book of prime entry but also part of the general ledger in which case the credit entry for the total column is not required.

Double entry for discount received:

Debit	Payables ledger control account
Credit	Discount received
Credit	VAT

Postings

Cash payments book							
Date	Details	Cheque No	Total	VAT £	Payables ledger £	Cash purchases £	Post £
14/2	K Ellis	1152	80.00		80.00		
15/2	Hutt Ltd	1153	120.00	20.00		100.00	
16/2	Biggs Ltd	1154	200.00				200.00
			400.00	20.00	80.00	100.00	200.00

Debit VAT account

Debit payables ledger control account

Debit cash purchases

Debit post

Posting the discounts received day book

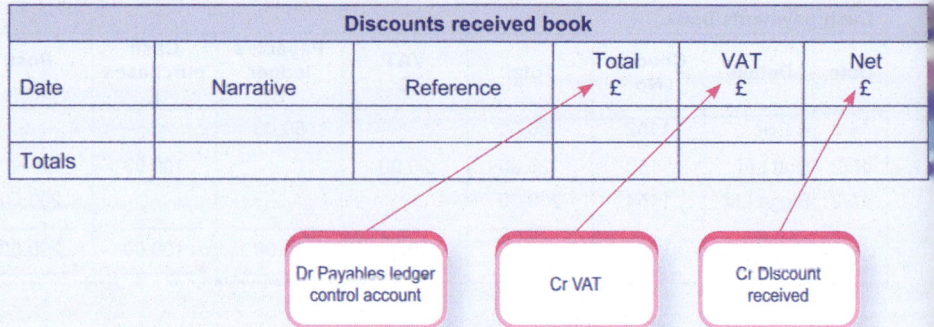

Discounts received book					
Date	Narrative	Reference	Total £	VAT £	Net £
Totals					

Dr Payables ledger control account

Cr VAT

Cr Discount received

Posting the cash payments book and discounts received book to the subsidiary ledger

- after the totals have been posted to the general ledger from the cash payments book the individual entries in the purchase ledger column must be posted to the subsidiary payables ledger

- each cash payment is debited to the individual payable account (reduction of amount owing)

- each discount received is debited to the individual payable account (reduction of amount owing).

Subsidiary payables ledger – postings (extracts)

K Ellis payment of £80.00 was detailed in the cash payments book. A discount received of £2.00 (gross) was also recorded.

K Ellis

	£	£
CPB	80.00	
DRB	2.00	

The cash book as part of the general ledger

The two sides of the cash book which are the cash receipts and the cash payments have been reviewed already as separate books.

The assessment often shows the cashbook as a ledger account format. This means that the cashbook actually forms a part of the general ledger, with the entries being one side of the double entry required within the general ledger.

The requirement will be to complete the other side of the entry within the general ledger, and to update the individual accounts in the subsidiary ledger.

KAPLAN PUBLISHIN

Petty cash system

Most businesses require small amounts of cash for small cash expenses and reimbursement of business expenditure incurred by employees.

Employee incurs expense e.g. purchase stamps for office

⬇

Fills out petty cash voucher for amount and attaches receipt

⬇

Takes to petty cashier who checks voucher and receipt and authorises voucher

⬇

Petty cashier gives employee amount spent out of petty cash box and puts voucher in petty cash box

⬇

Voucher is recorded in petty cash book

Petty cash box

- must be locked
- only petty cashier has access.

Imprest system

- most common system of controlling petty cash
- set amount of petty cash for period determined e.g. £100 per week
- cash paid out only when vouchers put into petty cash box
- at end of week petty cash box topped back up to £100 from bank account.

Monday	Friday	Friday
Petty cash box	Petty cash box	Petty cash box
£100 cash	£30 cash £70 vouchers	£100 (£70 withdrawn in cash from bank account. Vouchers removed and filed).

Non-imprest system

- another system of dealing with petty cash
- for example a set amount, say £100, being withdrawn in cash and put into the petty cash box each week no matter how much is paid out.

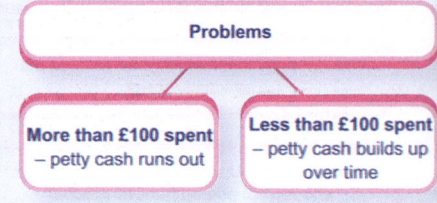

Problems

More than £100 spent – petty cash runs out

Less than £100 spent – petty cash builds up over time

Petty cash vouchers

- gives details of expenditure incurred by employee
- must normally be supported by receipt or other evidence of expense
- must include VAT for expense where VAT is reclaimable
- must be authorised before payment can be made.

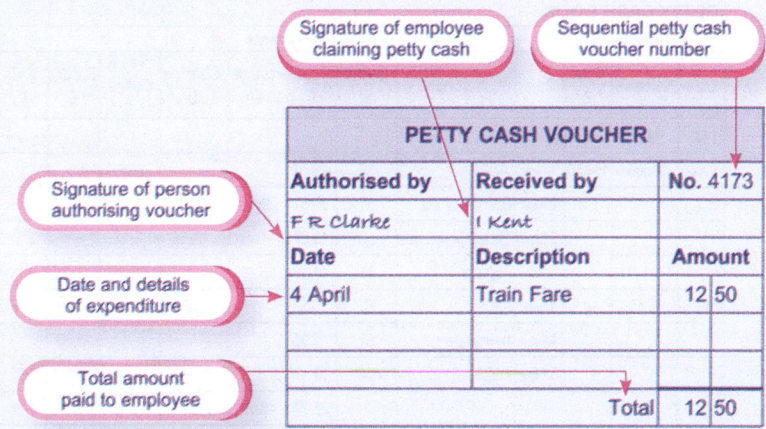

Signature of employee claiming petty cash

Sequential petty cash voucher number

Signature of person authorising voucher

Date and details of expenditure

Total amount paid to employee

PETTY CASH VOUCHER		
Authorised by	**Received by**	No. 4173
F R Clarke	I Kent	
Date	**Description**	**Amount**
4 April	Train Fare	12 50
	Total	12 50

Petty cash book

- book of prime entry
- often part of general ledger as well
- small cash receipts side
- larger analysed cash payments side.

PETTY CASH BOOK											
Receipts			**Payments**								
Date	Narrative	Total £	Date	Narrative	Voucher no	Total £	Postage £	Cleaning £	Tea & Coffee £	Sundry £	VAT £
1 Nov	Bal b/f	35.50									
1 Nov	Cheque	114.50	1 Nov	ASDA	58	23.50			23.50		
			2 Nov	Post Office Ltd	59	29.50	29.50				
			2 Nov	Cleaning materials	60	15.07		12.56			2.51
			3 Nov	Postage	61	16.19	16.19				
			3 Nov	ASDA	62	10.57		8.81			1.76
			4 Nov	Newspapers	63	18.90				18.90	
			5 Nov	ASDA	64	12.10				10.09	2.01
						125.83	45.69	21.37	23.50	28.99	6.28

Receipts side – only one column as only entry is regular payment in cash from bank

Payments side – analysed according to typical expenditure plus VAT column

Imprest amount of £150 to start week

Date of claim

Details

Sequential petty cash voucher numbers

Analysed payments – total column includes VAT but analysis column amount is net of VAT

When petty cash book has been written up for a period it must be totalled. Totals should then be checked by cross-casting:

	£
Postage	45.69
Cleaning	21.37
Tea & coffee	23.50
Sundry	28.99
VAT	6.28
Total	125.83

Topping up the petty cash box

- at the end of the period (in this case a week) the petty cash box will be topped up to the imprest amount
- this is done by taking cash out of the bank account
- amount is total of the petty cash expenditure – £125.83
- petty cash box should then have imprest amount of £150 in order to start following week.

Posting the petty cash book (PCB)

Petty cash book part of general ledger

- petty cash book is normally part of the general ledger.

Receipt of cash

- debit entry already in petty cash book
- only posting required is a credit in the cash payments book for the cash taken out of the bank (this should have been done from cheque stub anyway).

Petty cash payments

- credit entry in petty cash book (total column £125.83)
- debit entries required for each expense account and VAT account.

Postage account

	£		£
PCB	45.69		

Cleaning account

	£		£
PCB	21.37		

Food and drink account

	£		£
PCB	23.50		

Sundry expenses account

	£		£
PCB	28.99		

VAT account

	£		£
PCB	6.28		

Petty cash book not part of general ledger

- if the petty cash book is not part of the general ledger then a petty cash control account is required in the general ledger.

Petty cash receipt

- receipt of cash at start of week

Debit	Petty cash control account	£114.50
Credit	Bank account	£114.50

Petty cash payments

Debit	Postage	£45.69
	Cleaning	£21.37
	Food and drink	£23.50
	Sundry expenses	£28.99
	VAT	£ 6.28
Credit	Petty cash control account	£125.83

Reconciling petty cash

Under imprest system:

Therefore to check petty cash security:

- total cash in box
- total vouchers in box
- add together
- should equal imprest amount
- vouchers then removed from box, entered into petty cash book and filed.

Petty cash control account

If the petty cash book is not part of the general ledger there will be a petty cash control account in the general ledger which shows the summarised cash receipts and payments for the period.

Example

A petty cash system is run on an imprest system of £100. During the month of May petty cash expenditure totalled £68 and the petty cash box was topped back up to the imprest amount with a withdrawal of £68 cash from the bank.

Step 1 – Enter the imprest amount that would have been in the petty cash box at the start of the month – asset – debit balance.

Petty cash control account

	£		£
Opening balance	100		

Step 2 – Enter the total paid out in the month.

Petty cash control account

	£		£
Opening balance	100	Petty cash payments	68

Full double entry:

Debit   Expense accounts
Credit   Petty cash control account

Step 3 – Enter the cash paid into petty cash from the bank.

Petty cash control account

	£		£
Opening balance	100	Petty cash payments	68
Cash	68		

Full double entry:

Debit   Petty cash control account
Credit   Cash payments book

Step 4 – Carry down the balance at the end of the month – the imprest amount.

Petty cash control account

	£		£
Opening balance	100	Petty cash payments	68
Cash	68	Balance c/d	100
	168		168
Balance b/d	100		

Asset – debit balance

Topping up the petty cash box

- at the end of the period (in this case a week) the petty cash box will be topped up to the imprest amount
- this is done by taking cash out of the bank account
- amount is total of the petty cash expenditure – £68.00
- petty cash box should then have imprest amount of £100 in order to start following week.

Petty cash control account reconciliation

- at the end of a period the balance on the petty cash control account should equal the amount of cash in the petty cash box
- any difference must be investigated.

Differences

More cash than balance

- error in writing up petty cash book
- less cash given out than should have been

Less cash than balance

- error in writing up cash book
- too much cash given out than should have been
- petty cash voucher omitted from petty cash book
- cash paid out without voucher
- cash could have been stolen

8

Errors and suspense accounts

- What is a trial balance?
- Errors.
- Journal entries.
- Suspense account.
- Correcting errors and clearing the suspense account.

What is a trial balance?

- list of all of the ledger balances in the general ledger
- debit balances and credit balances listed in separate columns
- the total of the debit balances should equal the total of the credit balances.

Example

Trial balance

	Debit balances £	Credit balances £
Sales		5,000
Wages	100	
Purchases	3,000	
Rent	200	
Car	3,000	
Receivables	100	
Payables		1,400
	6,400	6,400

Debit or credit balance?

If you are just given a list of balances you must know whether they are debit or credit balances.

Remember the rules!

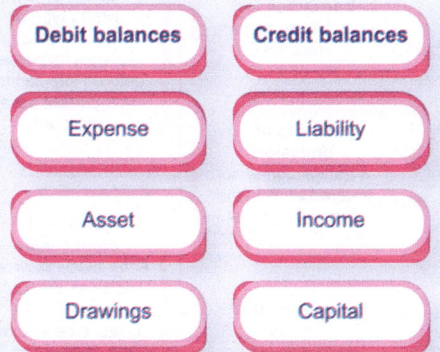

Debit balances	Credit balances
Expense	Liability
Asset	Income
Drawings	Capital

Errors

In a manual accounting system errors will be made – some are identified by extracting a trial balance but others are not.

Errors not identified by extracting a trial balance

Errors of original entry
error made when transaction first entered into primary records

Errors of principle
entry made in fundamentally wrong type of account e.g. revenue expense entered into capital/non-current asset account

Single entry
only one side of an entry made

Casting error
account incorrectly balanced

Errors identified by extracting a trial balance

Errors of omission
a transaction is not entered at all in the primary records

Transposition error
numbers transposed in recording e.g. 98 shown as 89

Extraction error
account balance entered on trial balance as wrong figure

Errors of commission
entry made in wrong account although account of the correct type e.g. rent expense entered into electricity expense account

Compensation errors
two or more errors which are exactly equal and opposite

Did you know? A transposition error can be identified by the difference being exactly divisible by 9!

Journal entries

- written instruction to bookkeeper to put through a double entry which has not been sourced from the books of prime entry
- used for correction of errors/adjustments/ unusual items
- only used for adjusting double entry errors in the general ledger – not used for entries in the subsidiary receivables or payables ledgers.

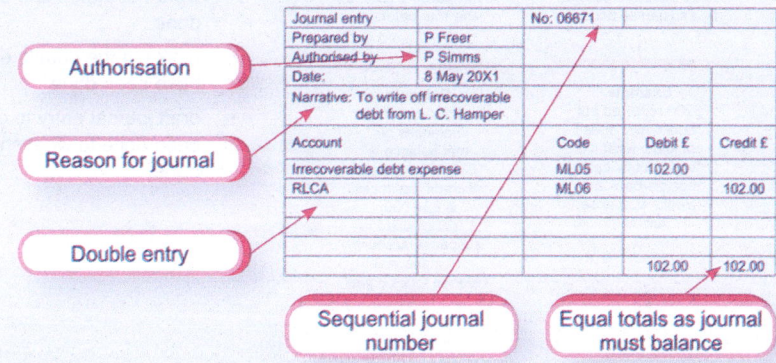

Journal entry		No: 06671		
Prepared by	P Freer			
Authorised by	P Simms			
Date:	8 May 20X1			
Narrative: To write off irrecoverable debt from L. C. Hamper				
Account		Code	Debit £	Credit £
Irrecoverable debt expense		ML05	102.00	
RLCA		ML06		102.00
			102.00	102.00

Authorisation

Reason for journal

Double entry

Sequential journal number

Equal totals as journal must balance

Suspense account

Used in two circumstances

Bookkeeper does not know one side of an entry therefore posts it to a suspense account

When trial balance totals disagree used to temporarily balance the trial balance

Example
£200 received but bookkeeper does not know what it is for so debits cash receipts book and credits suspense account

Example
Total of debit balances on trial balance is £35,000 but total of credit balances is £34,000. 1,000 credited to suspense account to make trial balance totals equal

Correcting errors and clearing the suspense account

- errors corrected by putting through a journal for the correcting entry.

How to find correcting entry

- work out the double entry that has been done

- work out the double entry that should have been done

- draft journal entry to go from what has been done to what should have been done.

9

Example

journal entries

(i) An amount of £200 for electricity bill payments was entered into the rent account.

What has been done?

Debit	Rent account	£200
Credit	Bank account	£200

What should have been done?

Debit	Electricity account	£200
Credit	Bank account	£200

How do we correct it? – Journal entry

Debit	Electricity account	£200
Credit	Rent account	£200

(ii) A purchase invoice for £1,000 had not been entered into the books of prime entry.

What has been done?

No entries at all

What should have been done?

Debit	Purchases account	£1,000
Credit	Payables ledger control account	£1,000

How do we correct it? – Journal entry

Debit	Purchases account	£1,000
Credit	Payables ledger control account	£1,000

(iii) An irrecoverable debt for £100 is to be written off.

This is not correction of an error but an adjustment to be made.

Journal entry

| Debit | Irrecoverable debt expense account | £100 |
| Credit | Receivables ledger control account | £100 |

(iv) A contra entry for £500 has been entered in the general ledger control accounts but has not been entered in the subsidiary payables ledger.

No journal entry is required as the error is not in the general ledger but the subsidiary ledger. However the payable's account in the subsidiary payables ledger must be debited to reflect this contra entry.

Errors and the suspense account

Some errors made will affect the trial balance and therefore are part of the suspense account balance.

Example

(i) Discounts allowed of £150 have been entered as a credit entry in the discounts allowed account

What has been done?

| Credit | Discount allowed account | £150 |
| Credit | Receivables ledger control account | £150 |

What should have been done?

| Debit | Discount allowed account | £150 |
| Credit | Receivables ledger control account | £150 |

How do we correct it? – Journal entry

| Debit | Discount allowed account | £300 |
| Credit | Suspense account | £300 |

The discount allowed account has been credited rather than debited with £150 therefore to turn this into a debit of £150 it needs to be debited with £300. No other account is incorrect so the other side of the entry is to the suspense account.

(ii) The balance for motor expenses of £400 has been omitted from the trial balance.

What has been done?

The motor expenses balance of £400 has been omitted from the trial balance.

What should be done?

A £400 debit balance (expense) must appear on the trial balance.

How do we correct it? – Journal entry

Debit	Motor expenses (TB)	£400
Credit	Suspense account	£400

Clearing the suspense account

The suspense account cannot remain as a permanent account and must eventually be investigated and cleared.

Example

A business has a suspense account with a debit balance of £80.

The following errors were noted:

(i) rent of £750 was entered into the rent account as £570

(ii) an advertising bill of was overstated in the advertising account by £100

Journals

(i) Debit   Rent account   £180

     Credit   Suspense account   £180

(ii) Debit   Suspense account   £100

     Credit   Advertising account   £100

Suspense account			
	£		£
Opening balance	80		
Advertising	100	Rent	180
	180		180

The suspense account is now cleared.

9

Control account reconciliations

- Receivables ledger control account.
- Receivables ledger control account reconciliation.
- Payables ledger control account.
- Payables ledger control account reconciliation.
- VAT control accounts.

Receivables ledger control account

- total receivables account
- sales invoices posted from sales day book
- credit notes posted from sales returns day book
- receipts from customers posted from cash receipts book.

Example

Writing up the Receivables ledger control account

The opening balance at 1 May on the Receivables ledger control account is £3,400.

Receivables ledger control account

	£		£
Opening balance	3,400		

Asset – debit balance

- total from sales day book for month of May £20,600

Receivables ledger control account

	£		£
Opening balance	3,400		
SDB	20,600		

Full double entry:

Debit   Receivables ledger control account

Credit Sales and VAT accounts

- total from sales returns day book for month of May £1,800

Receivables ledger control account

	£		£
Opening balance	3,400	SRDB	1,800
SDB	20,600		

Full double entry:

- **Debit** Sales returns and VAT accounts

- **Credit** Receivables ledger control account

- total from receivables column in cash receipts book of £19,500

Receivables ledger control account

	£		£
Opening balance	3,400	SRDB	1,800
SDB	20,600	CRB	19,500

Full double entry:

- **Debit** Cash book

- **Credit** Receivables ledger control account

- total of discounts allowed column in Discount allowed Daybook (DADB) £1,200.

Receivables ledger control account

	£		£
Opening balance	3,400	SRDB	1,800
SDB	20,600	CRB	19,500
		DADB	1,200

Full double entry:

Debit   **Discounts allowed account**

Credit   **Receivables ledger control account**

Other entries to the receivables ledger control account

There are two other potential entries in the receivables ledger control account:

- irrecoverable debts written off – when a debt is highly unlikely to be received
- contra entry – when money is owed to a supplier who is also a customer and therefore owes money – the two amounts are set off against each other.

Example

Irrecoverable debts written off

- a customer owing £400 has gone into liquidation and therefore it has been decided to write this debt off as bad.

Receivables ledger control account

	£		£
Opening balance	3,400	SRDB	1,800
SDB	20,600	CRB	19,500
		DADB	1,200
		Irrecoverable debt expense	400

Full double entry:

Debit   Irrecoverable debt expense account

Credit   Receivables ledger control account

Example continued – contra entry

- a customer who owes us £200 is also a supplier and we owe him £300. It has been agreed that the two amounts should be set off by a contra entry leaving only £100 owed by us to the supplier.

Receivables ledger control account

	£		£
Opening balance	3,400	SRDB	1,800
SDB	20,600	CRB	19,500
		DADB	1,200
		Irrecoverable debt write off	400
		Contra	200

Full double entry:

Debit   Payables ledger control account

Credit   Receivables ledger control account

> ### Example continued – balancing the receivables ledger control account
>
> #### Receivables ledger control account
>
> | | £ | | £ |
> |---|---|---|---|
> | Opening balance | 3,400 | SRDB | 1,800 |
> | SDB | 20,600 | CRB | 19,500 |
> | | | DADB | 1,200 |
> | | | Irrecoverable debt write off | 400 |
> | | | Contra | 200 |
> | | | Balance c/d | 900 |
> | | 24,000 | | 24,000 |
> | Balance b/d | 900 | | |
>
> This shows that at the end of May we have total receivables of £900.

Receivables ledger control account reconciliation

- the receivables ledger control account is written up using totals from the sales day book, sales returns day book and cash receipts book

- individual accounts for receivables in the subsidiary receivables ledger are written up using the individual entries from the sales day book, sales returns day book and cash receipts book

- as both are written up from the same sources of information, at the end of the period the balance on the sales ledger control account should equal the total of the list of balances in the subsidiary receivables ledger.

| RLCA balance | = | Total of list of subsidiary receivables ledger |

Purpose of receivables ledger control account reconciliation

- to show that RLCA does in fact equal the total of the list of balances

- to indicate that there are errors in either the RLCA or the subsidiary receivables ledger accounts if the two are not equal

- to find the correct figure for total receivables to appear in the trial balance.

Preparing a receivables ledger control account reconciliation

Step 1

- Extract list of balances from subsidiary receivables ledger accounts and total.

Step 2

- Balance the receivables ledger control account.

Step 3

- If the two figures are different the reasons for the difference must be investigated.

Step 4

- correct any errors that affect the receivables ledger control account
- find corrected balance on receivables ledger control account.

Step 5

- correct any errors that affect the total of the list of balances from the subsidiary receivables ledger
- find corrected total of list of subsidiary receivables ledger balances

Example

Receivables ledger control account reconciliation

The balance on the receivables ledger control account at 31 May is £4,100. The individual balances on the subsidiary receivables ledger are as follows:

	£
Receivable A	1,200
Receivable B	300
Receivable C	2,000
Receivable D	1,000

Step 1

- **Extract list of balances from subsidiary receivables ledger accounts and total**

	£
Receivable A	1,200
Receivable B	300
Receivable C	2,000
Receivable D	1,000
	4,500

Step 2

- **Balance the receivables ledger control account**

The balance has been given as £4,100.

Step 3

- **If the two figures are different the reasons for the difference must be investigated**

You are given the following information:

- a page of the sales day book had been undercast by £100

- a credit note for £50 to Receivable A had been entered into A's subsidiary receivables ledger account as an invoice

- a contra entry with Receivable B for £200 had only been entered in the receivables ledger control account and not the individual subsidiary receivables ledger account.

Step 4

- correct any errors that affect the receivables ledger control account
- find corrected balance on receivables ledger control account.

Receivables ledger control account

	£		£
Original balance	4,100		
SDB undercast	100	Correct balance	4,200
CPB	4,200		4,200
Correct balance	4,200		

If the sales day book was undercast then the amount posted to the receivables ledger control account was £100 too small and therefore an additional debit entry for £100 is needed in the control account.

The other two adjustments affect the individual accounts not the control account.

Step 5

- correct any errors that affect the total of the list of balances from the subsidiary receivables ledger
- find corrected total of list of subsidiary receivables ledger balances.

	£
Total list of balances	4,500
Less: Credit note entered as invoice	(100)
Less: Contra	(200)
Corrected list of balances	4,200

As the credit note for £50 had been entered as an invoice, the list of balances must be reduced by £100 to reflect the removal of the invoice and the entry of the credit note.

The contra had only been entered in the receivables ledger control account therefore £200 must be deducted from the list of balances.

Credit balances on receivables ledger accounts

- normally a receivable's balance on his subsidiary receivables ledger account will be a debit balance brought down

- sometimes however balance will be a credit balance.

Reasons for credit balance:

Overpayment by receivable

Misposting to subsidiary receivables ledger account

Treatment of credit balance

- when the list of subsidiary receivables ledger balances is drawn up and totalled, the credit balance must be deducted rather than added.

Payables ledger control account

- total payables account
- purchase invoices posted from purchases day book
- credit notes posted from purchases returns day book
- payments to suppliers posted from cash payments book
- discounts received from discount received day book.

Writing up the payables ledger control account

- the opening balance at 1 May on the payables ledger control account is £2,100

Payables ledger control account

£		£
	Opening balance	2,100

Liability – credit balance

- total from purchases day book for month of May £15,800

Payables ledger control account

	£		£
		Opening balance	2,100
		PDB	15,800

Full double entry:

Debit   Purchases and VAT accounts

Credit   Payables ledger control account

- total from purchases returns day book for month of May £900

Payables ledger control account

	£		£
PRDB	900	Opening balance	2,100
		PDB	15,800

Full double entry:

Debit   Payables ledger control account

Credit   Purchases returns and VAT accounts

- total from payables column in cash payments book of £13,000

Payables ledger control account

	£		£
PRDB	900	Opening balance	2,100
CPB	13,000	PDB	15,800

Full double entry:

Debit Payables ledger control account

Credit Cash Book

- total of discount received column in discount received daybook £700

Payables ledger control account

	£		£
PRDB	900	Opening balance	2,100
CPB	13,000	PDB	15,800
DRDB	700		

Full double entry:

Debit Payables ledger control account

Credit Discount received account

- a customer who owes us £200 is also a supplier and we owe him £300. It has been agreed that the two amounts should be set off by a contra entry leaving only £100 owed by us to the supplier.

Payables ledger control account

	£		£
PRDB	900	Opening balance	2,100
CPB	13,000	PDB	15,800
DRDB	700		
Contra	200		

Full double entry:

Debit Payables ledger control account

Credit Receivables ledger control account

Balancing the payables ledger control account

Payables ledger control account

	£		£
PRDB	900	Opening balance	2,100
CPB	13,000	PDB	15,800
DRDB	700		
Contra	200		
Balance c/d	3,100		
	17,900		17,900
		Balance b/d	3,100

This shows that we have payables totalling £3,100 at the end of May.

Payables ledger control account reconciliation

- the payables ledger control account is written up using totals from the purchases day book, purchases returns day book and cash payments book

- individual accounts for payables in the subsidiary payables ledger are written up using the individual entries from the purchases day book, purchases returns day book and cash payments book

- as both are written up from the same sources of information then at the end of the period the balance on the payables ledger control account should equal the total of the list of balances in the subsidiary payables ledger.

PLCA balance = Total of list of subsidiary payables ledger

Purpose of payables ledger control account reconciliation

- to show that the PLCA does in fact equal the total of the list of balances

- to indicate that there are errors in either the PLCA or the subsidiary payables ledger accounts if the two are not equal

- to find the correct figure for total payables to appear in the trial balance.

Preparing a payables ledger control account reconciliation

Step 1

- Extract list of balances from subsidiary payables ledger accounts and total.

Step 2

- Balance the purchases ledger control account.

Step 3

- If the two figures are different the reasons for the difference must be investigated.

Step 4

- correct any errors that affect the payables ledger control account
- find corrected balance on the payables ledger control account.

Step 5

- correct any errors that affect the total of the list of balances from the subsidiary payables ledger
- find corrected total of list of subsidiary payables ledger balances.

Example

Payables ledger control account reconciliation

The balance on the payables ledger control account at 31 May is £2,000. The individual balances on the subsidiary payables ledger are as follows:

	£
Payable E	800
Payable F	600
Payable G	400
Payable H	700

Step 1

- **Extract list of balances from subsidiary payables ledger accounts and total**

	£
Payable E	800
Payable F	600
Payable G	400
Payable H	700
	2,500

Step 2

- **Balance the payables ledger control account**

  The balance has been given as £2,000.

Step 3

- **If the two figures are different the reasons for the difference must be investigated.**

You are given the following information:

- a page of the purchases returns day book had been overcast by £1,000

- discounts received from suppliers totalling £680 had not been posted to the control account

- an invoice to payable G for £350 had been entered into the individual account in the subsidiary payables ledger as £530.

Step 4

- correct any errors that affect the payables ledger control account
- find corrected balance on payables ledger control account.

Payables ledger control account

	£		£
Discounts received	680	Original balance	2,000
Corrected balance	2,320	PRDB overcast	1,000
	3,000		3,000
		Corrected balance	2,320

If the purchases returns day book was overcast then the amount posted to the payables ledger control account on the debit side for returns was £1,000 too big

and therefore an additional credit entry for £1,000 is needed in the control account.

The discount received of £680 were omitted from the control account therefore the control account must be debited with this amount.

Step 5

- correct any errors that affect the total of the list of balances from the subsidiary payables ledger
- find corrected total of list of subsidiary payables ledger balances.

	£
Total list of balances	2,500
Less: transposition error on invoice (530 – 350)	(180)
Corrected total list of balances	2,320

The invoice had been entered as £180 higher than it should have been and therefore the total of the list of balances must be reduced by £180.

Example

Receivables ledger control account reconciliation

	£
Balance per receivables ledger control account	4,580
Total of list of subsidiary receivables ledger balances	4,780
Difference	200

In this case the list of balances is £200 higher than the control account total. What may have caused this?

Suppose that one balance in the list of balances is for £100. It is possible that this is in fact a credit balance of £100 but has been incorrectly added into the list of balances rather than being deducted.

Alternatively, if the control account includes an irrecoverable debt write off of £200, then it is possible that this has not been entered into the individual account in the subsidiary receivables ledger, causing the subsidiary receivables ledger balances to be higher than the control account balance.

VAT control accounts

As the sales, sales returns, purchases and purchases returns are entered into the accounts, the VAT is also calculated and accounted for.

You may be given extracts from the day books and asked to enter the relevant figures into the VAT control account, or you may be asked to list the entries required to the control account indicating whether they would be on the debit or credit side of the VAT control account.

It may also be a requirement to find the overall balance of the VAT control account i.e. to state what the balance is and whether it is owed to the tax authorities (HMRC) or whether a refund is due from them. The illustration above has shown us the VAT control account assuming that the balance brought down is on the credit side and therefore a liability. Although it is less likely, you may also encounter a VAT control account where the balance brought down is on the debit side and therefore an asset, meaning a refund is due to the business from the tax authorities.

VAT control account

	£		£
VAT on credit purchases		VAT on credit sales	
VAT on cash purchases		VAT on cash sales	
VAT on sales returns		VAT on purchases returns	
Balance c/d			
	___		___
	___	Balance b/d	___

10

Payroll procedures

- Gross pay and deductions.
- Total wages cost.
- Paying wages and salaries.
- Accounting for wages and salaries.
- Paying PAYE and NIC.

Gross pay and deductions

Gross pay

Made up of:

Basic wage + overtime + bonus + shift payment + commission etc

Net pay

	£
Gross pay	X
Less: PAYE	(X)
Less: Employee's NIC	(X)
Less: other deductions	(X)
Net pay to employee	X

PAYE

- deduction of income tax due on gross pay
- employer deducts correct amount of income tax for period from gross pay
- employer pays this income tax to HM Revenue and Customs (HMRC).

National Insurance Contributions (NIC)

- two types   – employee's NIC
                 – employer's NIC
- employee's NIC – deducted from gross pay by employer
                 – paid over to HMRC by employer
- employer's NIC – additional payment to HMRC by employer.

Other possible deductions

- pension contributions
- payments under save as you earn scheme (SAYE)
- payments under give as you earn scheme (GAYE)
- others such as subscriptions to sports/ social clubs, trade unions.

Total wages cost

Cost to employer = Gross pay + employer's NIC + employer's pension contributions

Paying wages and salaries

Cash
- very rare
- time-consuming
- security risk

Cheque
- time-consuming
- only practical for small number of employees

Methods of paying wages and salaries

Bank giro credit
- transfer directly to employee's bank account

BACS
- most common method
- transactions recorded on magnetic tape/ disc
- processed at BACS computer centre

Example

Gross pay of employee = £500 per week
PAYE = £100 for week
Employee's NIC = £80 for week
Employer's NIC = £90 for week

	£	
Gross pay	500	
Less: PAYE	(100)	Paid by employer to HMRC
Less: Employee's NIC	(80)	Paid by employer to HMRC
Employee's net pay	320	Paid to employee

Employer pays:

	£
Net pay to employee	320
PAYE to HMRC	100
Employee's NIC to HMRC	80
Employer's NIC to HMRC	90
Total cost to employer	590

Total wages cost to employer:

	£
Gross pay	500
Employer's NIC	90
	590

Accounting for wages and salaries

Example

Double entry

Gross pay of employee	= £500 per week
PAYE	= £100 for week
Employee's NIC	= £80 for week
Employer's NIC	= £90 for week

Step 1 – Gross pay

Debit Wages expense account £590
Credit Wages and salaries control £590
account

Double entry – two fundamentals

Cost to employer = gross pay + employer's NIC + employer's pension contributions

PAYE and NIC deductions paid over to HMRC by employer

The wages and salaries control account is used to ensure that all wages and salaries costs are correctly paid out to the appropriate parties

Wages expense account

	£		£
Wages and salaries control	590		

Wages and salaries control account

	£		£
		Wages expense	590

Step 2 – net pay

Debit	Wages and salaries control account (£500 – £100 – £80)	£320
Credit	Bank account	£320

Wages expense account

	£		£
Wages and salaries control	590		

Wages and salaries control account

	£		£
Bank	320	Wages expense	590

Step 3 – deductions payable to HMRC

Debit	Wages and salaries control account (£100 + £80 + £90)	£270
Credit	PAYE/NIC account	£270

Wages expense account

	£		£
Wages and salaries control	590		

Wages and salaries control account

	£		£
Bank	320	Wages expense	590
PAYE/NIC	270		

PAYE/NIC account

	£		£
		Wages and salaries control	270

Overall result – balance accounts

Wages expense account

	£		£
Wages and salaries control	590		
		balance c/d	590
	590		590
balance b/d	590		

= total wages cost for period (debit balance = expense)

Wages and salaries control account

	£		£
Bank	320	Wages expense	590
PAYE/NIC	270		
	590		590

= no balance – simply a control account.

PAYE/NIC

	£		£
Balance c/d	270	Wages and salaries control	270
	270		270
		Balance b/d	270

= amount due to HMRC
(credit balance = liability).

Paying PAYE and NIC

- payment of amounts deducted and due for PAYE, employee's and employer's NIC made each month
- made by bank giro credit to HM Revenue and Customs
- one payment covering all employees.

Double entry

Debit	PAYE/NIC account
Credit	Bank account

PAYE/NIC account

	£		£
		Wages and salaries control	270
Balance c/d	270		
	270		270
Bank	270	Balance b/d	270

11

Bank reconciliations

- Calculating the balance on the cash book.
- Comparing the cash book and the bank statement.
- Bank reconciliation statement.

Calculating the balance on the cash book

If a separate cash receipts book and cash payments book are used then the balance on the cash book at the end of the period is:

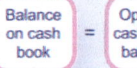 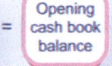

| Balance on cash book | = | Opening cash book balance | + | Cash book receipts total | − | Cash book payments total |

Example

A business had a balance on its cash book at 1 May of £750 debit. During May the cash receipts book shows a total of £5,340 and the cash payments book shows a total of £5,720.

Balance on cash book at end of May
= £750 + £5,340 − £5,720
= £370

Example

A business had a balance on its cash book at 1 May of £750 but this time it was a credit balance or overdraft balance. During May the cash receipts book shows a total of £5,340 and the cash payments book shows a total of £5,720.

Balance on cash book at end of May
= -£750 + £5,340 - £5,720
= £1,130 overdraft

Comparing the cash book and the bank statement

When the bank statement is received it should be checked to the cash book to ensure the accuracy of the cash book.

Debits and credits on bank statement

- a debit on the bank statement is a payment
- a credit on the bank statement is a deposit
- this is the opposite way round to the business ledger account as the bank statement is prepared from the bank's point of view.

Procedure

Step 1

- tick off items found in both cash book and on bank statement.

Step 2

- consider the unticked items in cash book and bank statement.

Unticked items in cash book

Items in cash book but not on bank statement

Outstanding lodgements Cheques paid into bank but not on bank statement yet	Unpresented cheques Cheques written by business but not cleared onto bank statement	Errors in cash book which cannot be matched to bank statement

Unticked items on bank statement

Direct debits/ standing orders

payments made directly out of the bank which have not been entered into cash payments book

Direct credits/ BACS receipts

credits directly into the bank account which have not yet been entered into cash receipts book

Items on bank statement but not in cash book

Bank charges/ interest

not yet in cash book as cashier does not know about them until bank statement received

Errors in cash book

errors such as transposition errors which only come to light when cash book is compared to bank statement

Bank reconciliation statement

Step 1 **Compare cash book to bank statement**

- covered above.

Step 2 **Enter items which are on bank statement but not yet in cash book into the cash book**

- typical items include bank charges, direct debits, direct credits or standing orders

- correct any errors in the cash book.

Step 3 **Balance amended cash book**

- this should give the correct balance on the cash book

- this will not usually agree with the bank statement balance due to timing differences.

Step 4 **Prepare bank reconciliation statement**

Bank reconciliation statement

	£
Balance per bank statement	X
Less: unpresented cheques	(X)
Add: outstanding lodgements	X
Balance per cash book	X

Once the unpresented cheques and outstanding lodgements have been taken into account the bank statement balance should agree to the amended cash book balance. The cash book and bank statement are reconciled.

Example

A company's cashier has compared the cash book for the month of May to the bank statement at 31 May. The following differences have been noted:

- bank charges of £35 on the bank statement not in cash book
- direct debit of £100 on bank statement not in cash book
- cheques written by the business totalling £340 not yet on bank statement
- cheques paid into bank account totalling £200 not yet on bank statement.

The balance on the cash book before this reconciliation took place was a debit balance of £700 but the balance on the bank statement was £705 in credit.

Amend cash book

Cash book

	£		£
Original balance	700	Bank charges	35
		Direct debit	100
		Amended closing balance	565
	700		700
Amended cash book balance	565		

Prepare bank reconciliation statement

	£
Balance per bank statement	705
Less: unpresented cheques	(340)
Add: outstanding lodgements	200
Balance per cash book	565

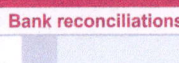

12

The English legal system

- Definition of law.
- Sources of law.
- Judicial precedent.
- Remedies.
- Types of law.
- Criminal law v civil law.
- Court system.

Definition of law

The principles and regulations established in a community by some authority and applicable to its people whether in the form of legislation or of custom and policies recognised and enforced by judicial decision.

Sources of law

Case law	Legislation
Common law <ul><li>Introduced the system of precedent.</li><li>The only remedy was damages.</li><li>Rigid and inflexible.</li></ul>	**Direct legislation** = Acts of Parliament. A Bill must go through the following stages in both the House of Lords and the House of Commons: 1st reading, 2nd reading, committee stage, report stage, 3rd reading, Royal Assent.
Equity <ul><li>Began as a form of appeal.</li><li>More flexible than the common law.</li><li>Introduced new discretionary remedies such as injunctions and specific performance.</li><li>Concerned with fairness.</li></ul>	**Indirect legislation** = delegated legislation. Consists of: <ul><li>**Statutory instruments** – Made by Government Ministers using powers delegated by Parliament</li><li>**Bye-laws** – Made by local authorities</li><li>**Orders in Council** – Made by the Privy Council in the name of the Monarch on the advice of the Prime Minister.</li></ul>

Judicial precedent

Ratio decidendi	Obiter dicta
The legal reason for the decision	Statements which are not part of the ratio
The ratio is capable of forming the binding precedent	Persuasive rather than binding precedent

Advantages of judicial precedent – consistency, flexibility, practical.

Disadvantages – complex, restricts judges' discretion. However, judges retain discretion by 'distinguishing on the facts' or overruling lower courts.

Remedies

Damages = monetary compensation awarded by a court to an individual who has suffered the wrongful conduct of another party. They are a common law remedy.

Equitable remedies

Specific Performance	The defendant is ordered to carry out their contractual duties.
Injunction	A court order requiring a person to do or cease to do a specific action.
Rescission	The cancellation of a contract.

Types of law

Public law	Private law
Deals with matters relating to whole country e.g. criminal law, constitutional law and administrative law.	Deals with law enforced between individuals e.g. contract and family law.

Criminal law v civil law

Criminal law	Civil law
Criminal law relates to conduct which the State considers with disapproval and which it seeks to control.	Civil law is a form of private law and involves the relationships between individual citizens.
Purpose is the enforcement of particular forms of behaviour by the State, which acts to ensure compliance.	Purpose is to settle disputes between individuals and to provide remedies.
In criminal law the case is brought by the State in the name of the Crown. A criminal case will be reported as Rex v ..., where Rex means the latin for 'king'.	In civil law the case is brought by the claimant, who is seeking a rememdy. The case will be referred to by the names of the parties involved in the dispute, such as Brown v Smith.
Burden of proof – on the prosecution.	**Burden of proof – on the claimant.**
Standard of proof – guilt must be shown **beyond reasonable doubt**.	**Standard of proof** – liability must be shown on the **balance of probabilities**.
Object – to regulate society by the threat of punishment.	Object – usually financial compensation to put the claimant in the position they would have been in had the wrong not occurred.
If found guilty the criminal court will sentence the defendant and it may fine them or impose a period of imprisonment. If innocent the accused will be acquitted.	The civil court will order the defendant to pay damages or it may order some other remedy, e.g. specific performance or injunction.

Court system

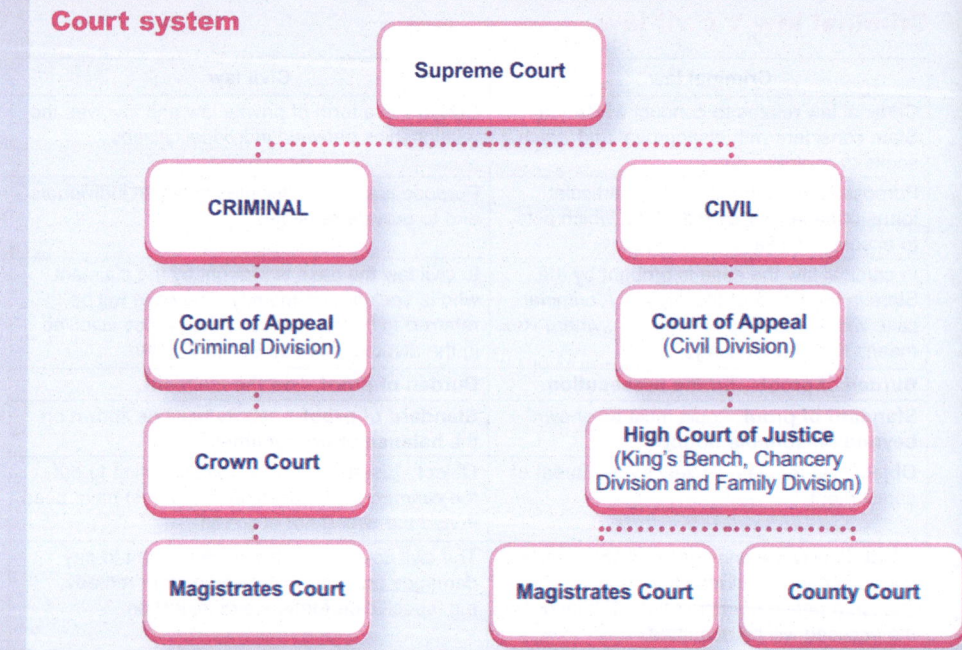

13

Contract law

- Offer.
- Acceptance.
- Consideration.
- Intention to create legal relations.
- Capacity and legality.
- Types of contracts.
- Discharging a contract.
- Remedies.
- Consumer Rights Act 2015.

Offer

Definition

An offer is a definite and unequivocal statement of willingness to be bound on specified terms without further negotiations. Once accepted it forms a valid contract.

It can be made to a particular person, to a class of persons or even to the whole world: **Carlill v Carbolic Smoke Ball Co**.

What is not an offer?

- A mere statement of selling price in response to a request for info.
- An invitation to treat = an invitation to the other party to make an offer.

Examples of invitations to treat

- Most adverts
- Shop window displays
- Goods on shop shelves

How does an offer terminate?

- **Revocation** by the offeror at any time before acceptance, even if agreed to keep open. However, must be communicated to offeree by offeror or reliable third party.
- **Rejection** by the offeree – either outright or by a counter-offer.
- **Lapse** – on death of offeror or offeree, or after expiry of fixed time.

Acceptance

Acceptance is the unqualified and unconditional assent to all the terms of an offer. It can be oral, written or by conduct.

A **counter offer** is an offer made in response to a previous offer. Making a counter offer automatically terminates the prior offer and requires an acceptance under the terms of the counter offer or there is no contract.

Subject to contract = the parties are not legally bound until a contract has been executed.

Consideration

The exchange of value between the parties in a contract is known as consideration. In essence both parties must have agreed to provide something of value to each other.

The consideration needs to satisfy the following criteria:

Sufficient	It must be of some value (usually monetary), even if it is a minimal value. It does not have to be adequate, i.e. represent the true value of the exchange. For example if £100 was paid for some land worth £50,000, the £100 would still be valid consideration.
Legal	The exchange should not be against the law.
Timely	Consideration must not be past i.e something that has already been provided at the time the contract is made. It must be exchanged at the time the contract is made, or afterwards (see below).
Executed Or Executory	The consideration is carried out at the time the contract is made. For example, handing over 60p and receiving a newspaper.
	An exchange of promises to do something in the future. For example, when there is an agreement to pay for goods 'cash on delivery'. The payment and the delivery are 'executory' – completed at a later date.

Intention to create legal relations

A contract does not exist unless the parties intend it to be legally enforceable. The law presumes the intention of the parties based on the type of agreement. The presumption can be rebutted by clear evidence to the contrary.

Domestic or social agreements	Commercial agreements
Presume no intention to be legally bound.	Presume intention to be legally bound.

Capacity and legality

Capacity	In order to enter into a contract, the parties must have capacity.
	The following are considered to have limitations on their power to contract and would not be bound to some types of contracts (e.g. financial contracts such as loan agreements):
	• Minors – persons under the age of 18 years old
	• Persons of unsound mind
	• Anyone under the influence of alcohol or drugs.
Legality	A contract must be for a legal purpose.

Types of contracts

Void	Cannot be enforced by law.
Voidable	A valid contract that can be made legally null and void by one party to the contract.

Discharging a contract

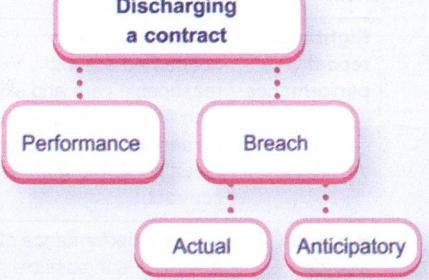

Remedies

Damages = monetary compensation awarded by a court to an individual who has suffered the wrongful conduct of another party. They are a common law remedy.

Equitable remedies

Specific Performance	The defendant is ordered to carry out their contractual duties.
Injunction	A court order requiring a person to do or cease to do a specific action.
Rescission	The cancellation of a contract.

Consumer Rights Act 2015

Covers what should happen when goods or digital content are faulty and how services should match up to what has been agreed.

Remedies for faulty goods

Up to thirty days	Immediate refund.
Up to six months	Right to have the item repaired or replaced. If the attempt to repair or replace the item is unsuccessful the consumer has the right to a refund or a price reduction.
Up to six years	If the goods do not last a reasonable length of time the consumer may be entitled to some money back.

Remedies for where a service has not been provided with reasonable care and skill

Right to repeat performance	Where a service is not carried out with reasonable care and skill then the service must be performed again so that it conforms with the contract.
Right to a price reduction	If repeat performance of a service is impossible or it cannot be carried out within a reasonable time or without causing significant inconvenience, then the consumer is entitled to a price reduction.

14

External business environment

- Economic environment.
- Demand and supply.
- Globalisation.
- Government control and influence.
- Competitive environment.

Economic environment

Microeconomics is the study of the economic behaviour of individual consumers, firms and industries. It focuses on how these three individual parts of an economy make decisions about how to allocate scarce resources.

Macroeconomics considers aggregate behaviour, and the sum of individual economic decisions – in other words, the workings of the economy as a whole.

Demand and supply

Demand shows how much of a good or service someone intends to buy at different prices.

Demand tends to be higher at a low price and lower at a high price for most goods and services.

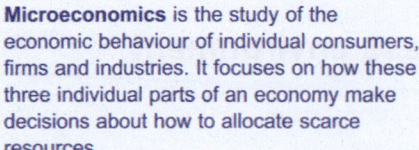

| **Substitution effect** | Where a consumer buys more of one good and less of another because of relative price changes. |
| **Income effect** | Where a change in the price of a good affects the purchasing power of the consumers' income (a change in their real income). |

Expansion = demand rises when the price falls

Contraction = demand falls when the price rises

What affects demand?

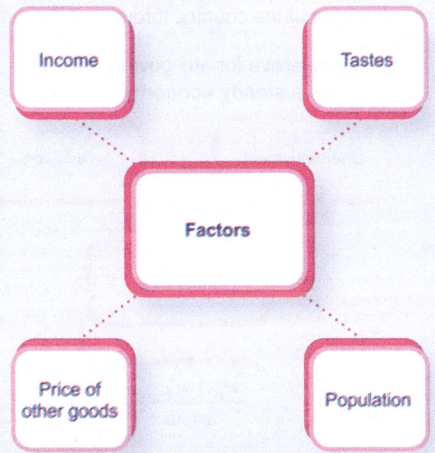

Income

Tastes

Factors

Price of other goods

Population

Supply

Definition

Supply shows how many units producers would be willing to offer for sale, at different prices, over a given period of time.

Decrease in supply = increase in production costs

Due to:

- higher production costs
- indirect taxes

Increase in supply = fall in production costs

Due to:

- technological innovations
- more efficient use of existing factors of production
- improvements in productivity
- lower input prices
- a reduction of an indirect tax

Globalisation

Globalisation is the process by which the world is becoming increasingly interconnected as a result of massively increased trade and cultural exchange.

Advantages	Disadvantages
Job creation	Creates inequality
Lower prices for consumers	Increases carbon footprint
Improved access to technology	
Improved productivity	

Government control and influence

An economy of a country is a collection of business transactions that take place throughout the country, throughout the year.

A key objective for any government is to maintain a **steady economy**.

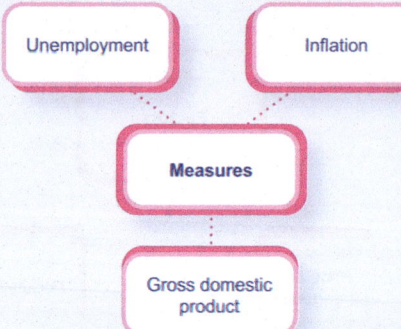

Fiscal policy is the use of government spending and/or taxation as a tool to influence the economy.

Expansionary fiscal policy = increase in government spending (or decrease in tax) in order to stimulate the economy.

Contractionary fiscal policy = decrease in government spending (or increase in tax) in order to cool the economy down during an economic boom.

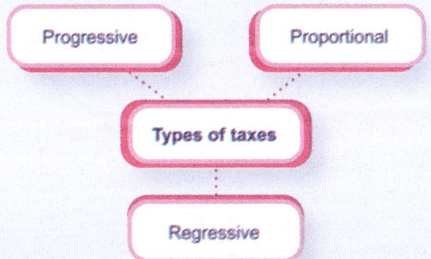

An **interest rate** determines the level of interest that is paid by someone who borrows money and the level of interest they receive if they save money.

An increase in interest rates will generally discourage people from spending, whereas a decrease in interest rates will encourage people to spend more. If consumers are spending more this will generate more growth in the economy which in turn will result in higher employment.

Competitive environment

Definition

The **exchange rate** tells us how currencies compare and also the price at which one currency can be traded for another.

If a country wants to import products, they'll pay for the products in the currency of the country it was made in.

A country's exchange rate can be affected by that particular country's economy as well as the global economy.

If the value of the pound sterling (£) decreases **(depreciation)**, this means that businesses will be able to buy less foreign currency for the same price as before. If a business buys products from overseas, this will result in a higher cost for them as those products will now be more expensive.

If the value of the pound sterling (£) increases **(appreciation)**, this means that it will become more expensive for businesses abroad to buy products from the UK. This in turn will lead to less demand for those products, causing a decrease in exports.

15

CSR, ethics and sustainability

- Ethical principles.
- Threats to ethical principles.
- Sustainability and corporate social responsibility.

Ethical principles

Confidentiality

Do not disclose information to third parties unless you have proper authority to do so, or that you have a legal or professional right or duty to disclose information.

Do not use information acquired as a result of your business or work activities for personal advantage, or pass on that information for others to gain a personal advantage.

This will include non-disclosure of information to others within your organisation e.g. not disclosing personal salary or contact details of a colleague to a co-worker.

Objectivity

All work activities should be undertaken without bias or conflict of interest so that they can be relied upon by others.

Definition

Ethics – a set of moral principles that governs the behaviour of individuals.

Professional competence and due care

Confidentiality

Objectivity

Ethical principles

Professional behaviour

Integrity

Professional competence and due care

Professional competence relates to having the underlying knowledge, skills and capabilities to perform your job. Due care relates to the application of knowledge, skills and capabilities when performing work.

If you fail to exercise due care in the performance of your work, potentially you will be regarded as being negligent.

Integrity

This relates to honesty and being straightforward in your dealings with others in the course of your work.

Professional behaviour

You should behave in such a way as to not bring disrepute upon yourself or your profession.

Threats to ethical principles

Self-interest

Objectivity may be threatened if your work or decision-making is compromised by having a personal interest in a transaction or event e.g. behaving in a way to give yourself or a friend or colleague a personal or financial benefit in a transaction or event.

Self-review

Objectivity may be compromised if you need to reconsider or review the results of your earlier work. You should not try to disguise or avoid making disclosure of errors or omissions in your work.

Advocacy

You should perform your work with an independent and objective manner, presenting information fully and in an impartial manner. Ideally, you should present full information and explanation to others so that they can make appropriate decisions.

If you are required to express a point of view or opinion on an issue, you should ensure that it is fully supported by factual information and that you present a balanced perspective, such as including references to possible risks or disadvantages of a particular course of action.

Familiarity

Objectivity may be compromised if you have undue familiarity with a situation or with the individuals involved. For example, you have been asked to investigate a particular transaction which appears to be unusual. Undue familiarity may be a problem if the colleague responsible for the transaction is a personal friend, or if you place too much reliance upon explanation and comment received, without proper consideration of what you have been told.

Intimidation

This risk to ethical behaviour may take several forms, such as financial intimidation by a customer threatening not to purchase goods from your organisation unless they are given preferential terms to which they are not entitled. It could also take the form of your manager requiring you to prepare information in a specified way that omits or disguises important details with the threat that, if you fail to comply, it may adversely affect your appraisal or salary grading. In rare cases, intimidation could be the threat of physical violence to you, family or colleagues.

Planning and foresight – if you become aware of any potential threats to ethical behaviour, you should advise your manager so that appropriate safeguards can be put in place to avoid or minimise any potential problem.

Similarly, it is not always possible to pre-empt all potential problems. If you become aware of an ethical problem that cannot be avoided, you should advise your manager so that appropriate action can be taken to minimise any potential problem.

Sustainability and corporate social responsibility

Sustainability – how to meet the needs of the present without compromising the ability of future generations to meet their own needs.

Corporate Social Responsibility – defined as a business approach that contributes to sustainable development by delivering economic, social and environmental benefits for all stakeholders. This is often referred to as 'The Three P's' – People, Planet and Profit.

The elements of 'People, Planet, and Profit' are inter-related. For example, upholding good ethical principles could apply to the relationships that people have in business, but could also relate to profit if upholding good ethical principles leads to increased profits over a period of time.

Note that implementing policies which promote sustainability may incur costs e.g. purchasing vehicles that are more fuel-efficient which may not necessarily be the lowest cost vehicle. However, many organisations now believe that socially responsible sustainability policies bring benefits, such as an enhanced business reputation along with improved employee morale and commitment. This, in turn, may lead to improved business efficiency and increased sales revenues from customers

who share similar values.

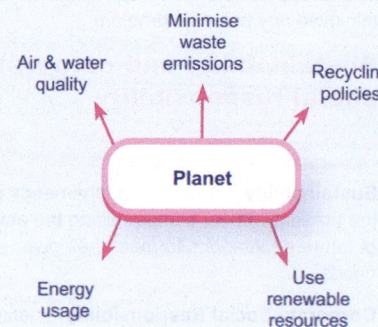

People

- Human rights and equality
- Flexible working practices
- Training and development policies
- Ethical principles
- Local community

Planet

- Air & water quality
- Minimise waste emissions
- Recycling policies
- Energy usage
- Use renewable resources

CSR initiatives – people (CSR)

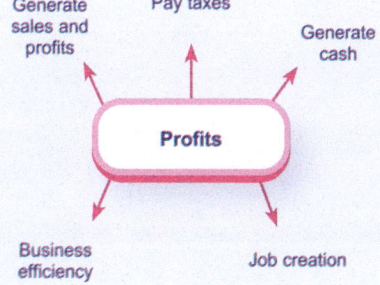

Generate sales and profits

Pay taxes

Generate cash

Profits

Business efficiency

Job creation

16

Different types of business entity

- Models of business ownership.
- Legal administration.
- Business formation.

Models of business ownership

Under the **entity concept**, transactions related to a business must be recorded separately from those of its owners and any other business.

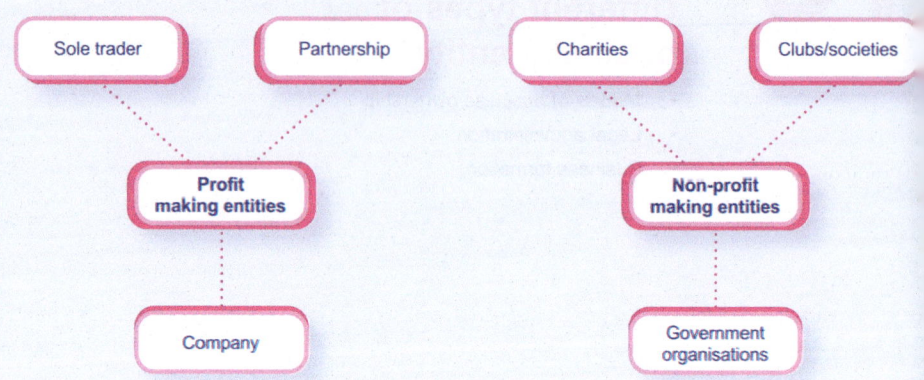

Tax implications

Company	Corporation tax, VAT and employer's NIC (all assessed on company)
Partnership	Income tax and national insurance contributions (assessed on partners) VAT and employer's NIC (partnership)
Sole trader	Income tax and national insurance contributions (assessed on sole trader) VAT and employer's NIC (business)

Limited liability

Shareholders have limited liability. In the event that the business fails, the shareholders will only be asked to contribute identifiable amounts to the assets of the business. The company itself is fully liable for its debts.

Sole traders and partnerships do not have limited liability. A sole trader or partner in a partnership are fully liable for the debts of the business.

Legal administration

Sole trader	No formal legal requirements.
	For tax purposes they will need to maintain records of business income and expenses including details of:
	• sales and income
	• expenses
	• VAT paid and charged (if VAT registered)
	• PAYE deducted from employee's salaries
	Records must be kept for five years from the deadline for the submission of the tax return for the period to which they relate.
Company	Maintain statutory registers:
	• members
	• directors and company secretary
	• charges
	• persons with significant control
	Also require:
	• confirmation statement
	• accounting records
	• annual accounts

Business formation

Sole trader	No legal formalities Needs to register with HMRC for self-assessment of income tax
Partnership	No legal formalities May have a partnership agreement Needs to register with HMRC to complete a partnership tax return The partners will need to register with HMRC for self-assessment of income tax
Company	Formal registration process with Companies House where the following need to be filed: • memorandum of association • application for registration • statement of capital • statement of consent to act • statement of compliance Register for corporation tax with HMRC

A **pre-incorporation contract** is a contract by a person acting on behalf of an unformed company

The legal position is that the person acting on behalf of the company is legally liable for the contract.

An 'off-the-shelf' company can be used:

Advantages	Disadvantages
Cheap and simple to buy.	Some documents will need to be submitted to Companies House which will need to be tailored to the company.
Can trade immediately.	May have unsettled liabilities.
No problem of pre-incorporation contracts.	
Can be more appealing to lenders.	

A business name must comply with the following rules:

- It cannot be the same as another in the index of names.
- It cannot use certain words which are illegal or offensive.
- It must have the Secretary of State's consent to use certain words (e.g. England, Chartered, Royal, National, University, Insurance etc.) or any name suggesting a connection with the government or any local authority.

The business name should be displayed on premises in a prominent position where customers and suppliers have access. It should also be included on a number of business documents.

An active company must display their full registered name at:

- their registered office
- all other locations at which they carry on business
- the place where company records are available for inspection.

17

The role of the finance function

- The functions of a business.
- The role of the finance function.
- How the finance team contributes to the success of a business.

The functions of a business

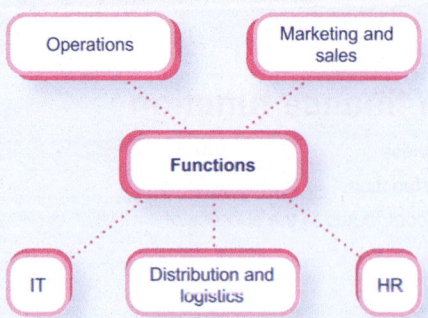

Operations

Marketing and sales

Functions

IT

Distribution and logistics

HR

The role of the finance function

Responsibilities which are relevant to **external stakeholders:**

- producing the statutory financial statements
- producing and filing other returns and documents required by law

Responsibilities which are relevant to **internal stakeholders:**

- banking of cash and receipts
- maintaining the accounting records and general ledger accounts
- producing information to assist and support other parts of the business
- producing management accounts and supporting information
- producing summaries and reconciliations

Examples of tasks and activities that may be outsourced:

- preparation of the monthly or quarterly returns for VAT
- preparation of the monthly or quarterly management accounts
- preparation of the annual tax return for the business and calculation of the amount due
- the internal audit function
- ad hoc investigation work, such as investigation of potential fraud or other irregulariities
- preparation of the weekly or monthly payroll, creation of individual payslips plus summaries and totals of the payroll cost and the associated liabilities

How the finance team contributes to the success of a business

Effective communication needs to be clear, complete, accurate, timely and concise. It also needs to meet the needs of the recipient. The means of communication should also be appropriate and match the needs of the recipient.

Efficient working practices require planning and understanding what information is required, when it is required, by whom and in what format to assist with control and decision-making in the business.

Financial accounting and management accounting

Financial accounting	Management accounting
Limited companies are required by law to prepare annual finacial statements	Records are not mandatory
The cost of record-keeping is a necessity	The cost of record-keeping needs to be justified
Objectives and uses are not defined by management	Objectives and uses are decided by management
Mainly a historial record	Concerned with future results as well as historical data
Information must be compiled and in accordance with legal and accounting requirements	Information should be compiled as management requires – the key criterion being relevance
Prepared for external reporting	Prepared for internal use only

Solvency

Solvency is the financial soundness of an organisation that allows it to discharge its monetary obligations (such as paying payables on time) as they fall due. To this end they must ensure that they have cash available to meet these obligations.

Ways to manage or improve solvency

- regular reconciliation of bank balances to highlight bank charges and interest, direct debit and standing order payments and BACS receipts from customers to monitor transactions passing through the bank account

- awareness of bank account balances to identify whether they may become overdrawn and to plan ways to avoid the overdraft or incur the changes and interest

- awareness of how much is owed to the organisation by maintaining a sales ledger control account

- awareness of how much is owed by the organisation by maintaining a purchase ledger control account, and other records such as loan liabilities and recognising when they are due for payment

- awareness and use of forward planning to identify whether there is a need to arrange for increased or extended credit or loan facilities to meet organisation needs

- awareness and use of forward planning to identify whether it is advantageous, and on what terms, to offer credit facilities and discounts to customers and whether it is beneficial to use credit facilities and discounts offered by suppliers.

Legal obligations

- Statutory financial statements
- VAT returns and payment dates
- Corporation tax
- **Legal obligations**
- Data protection
- Health and safety

Internal policies

- Annual leave policy
- Overtime and bonus payments
- Ethical principles
- **Internal policies**
- Absence notification
- Authorised signatories
- Expense claims

18

Business communication and planning

- Sources of information.
- Communication of information.
- Planning workloads.
- Planning methods.
- Difficulties in meeting deadlines.

Sources of information

Definition

Data is unorganised or unstructured facts or statistics. Data has no meaning unless it is arranged, structured or refined into information.

Definition

Information is data that is organised or structured and therefore provides context for understanding and decision-making.

Definition

Valid information is information that is reliable or credible. This could be in terms of accuracy or reasonableness when based upon assumptions or estimations.

Definition

Knowledge is the ability to use information to achieve objectives.

Primary sources of data are created at the time an event is occurring. Notes or minutes taken during a meeting is an example of a primary source of data.

Secondary sources of data are anything other than primary sources. Normally, it is not collected for a specific purpose and it may be used in a number of different ways or for different purposes.

Internal sources of data and information are obtained, as it suggests, from within the business.

External sources of data and information are obtained, as it suggests, from outside the business.

KAPLAN PUBLISHING

Communication of information

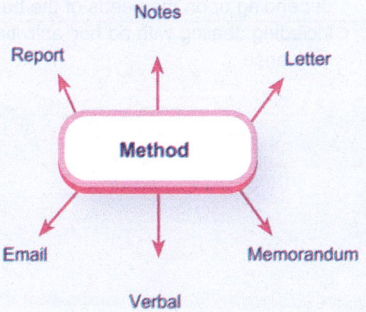

- Report
- Notes
- Letter
- **Method**
- Email
- Memorandum
- Verbal

Communication of information should be made in a timely, appropriate and professional manner. For example, any report, memorandum or email should be formatted and presented, perhaps with the use of headings, paragraphs and bullet points to provide structure. Professional business language should be used at all times.

Remember to consider confidentiality of information – do you have approval from a responsible person (e.g. your manager) to communicate information to another person (e.g. a supplier or the sales director) particularly if that information could be regarded as being personal or sensitive in any way?

Planning workloads

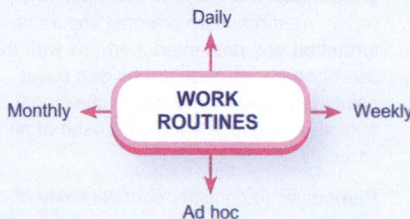

Planning requires not only identification of the tasks or duties to be performed within a given timescale, but also an estimate of the time each item will take. For longer-term planning, this will help to identify potential problems, and enable rescheduling of activities so that they can be achieved within required timescales.

For shorter-term planning, this may involve scheduling activities within the week or day ahead. They may need to be reorganised depending upon the needs of the business, including dealing with ad hoc activities that may arise.

Planning methods

Checklists

Bar charts

Activity / job schedules

PLANNING METHODS

Diaries – personal or organisation based

Planning boards / charts

Difficulties in meeting deadlines

One important point about planning is that it helps to identify potential problems before they arise. Potential problems can then be reported to an appropriate person so that action may be taken to avoid or minimise the problem. For example, bottlenecks and clashes of commitments can be identified and amended to remove the problem.

Problems may be unexpected, such as system crashes or a colleague absent due to illness. In these situations, current plans need to be reconsidered and amended, which may include amending priorities.

The role of information

- Information in the work of the finance function.
- The importance of data and information security.

Information in the work of the finance function

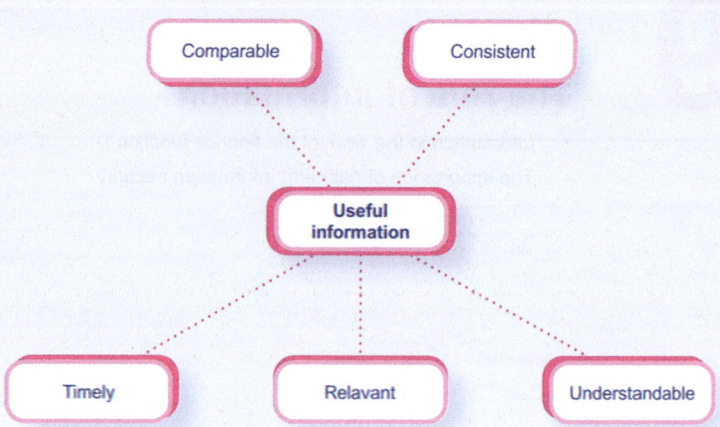

Digital technologies

Advantages	Disadvantages
Reduced operational costs	Capital costs of acquiring or developing the software
Human error recording data is reduced	Staff training costs
Rapid and easy capture of data	Reliance upon systems that may crash
Improved security of data	Security of data may be compromised
Improved ease of access to data	Loss or inadequacy of tracking and analytical capability to meet user needs
Improved ability to track and analyse data	
Environmental and commercial benefits from using less paper	

Cloud accounting is an accounting system that is accessed through the internet. This contrasts with desktop-based systems which require regular software updates, along with the cost of backing-up procedures.

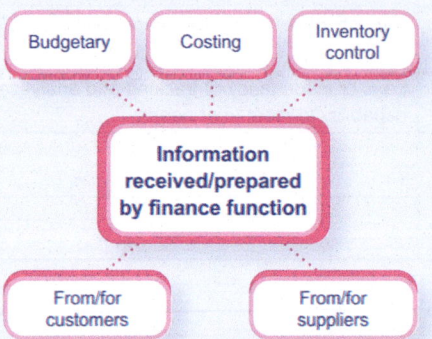

Other information produced by the finance function:

- cash and petty cash books, including supporting invoices, vouchers and receipts

- bank reconciliations and reconciliations of the petty cash balance

- lists of cash and cheque receipts

- summaries of the available cash balance

- accounting transactions and ledger accounts

- summaries of wages and salaries payments required each week or month, along with related returns and payments to HMRC

- preparing information and returns required by HMRC to support payments of VAT and other business taxes

The importance of data and information security

Definition

Cybersecurity is the application of processes, systems and controls to protect systems, networks, programs, devices and data from cyberattacks.

Definition

A **cyberattack** is an attempt to damage or destroy a computer network or system.

Risks to data:

- physical intrusion
- physical damage
- operational mistakes
- industrial espionage/fraud

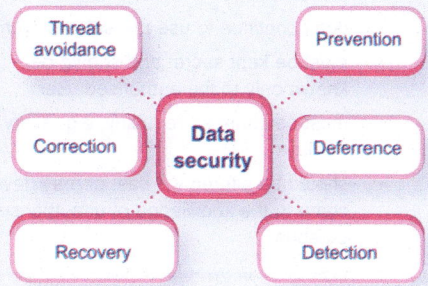

Password rules:

* must not be easy to guess
* should consist of at least one non-letter character (special character or number) and have at least six characters
* selection of trivial passwords must be prevented
* don't continue to use pre-set passwords
* must be kept secret and should be known only to the authorised user
* must be changed regularly, e.g. every 90 days
* should be altered if it has, or may have, come to the knowledge of unauthorised persons
* previous passwords should no longer be used and re-use of previous passwords should be prevented by the IT system

Definition

Hacking is an attempt to exploit a compute network or private network within a computer. It is unauthorised access to a system for an illicit purpose.

Relevant controls to help prevention:

* physical security
* authorisation
* passwords
* data encryption
* system logs
* random checks
* shielding of VDUs

Index

KAPLAN PUBLI